THE STUDY OF CELTIC LITERATURE

LECTOR HOUSE PUBLIC DOMAIN WORKS

THE STUDY OF CELTIC LITERATURE

MATTHEW ARNOLD

9 789356 146730
ISBN: 978-93-5614-673-0

Published: 1891

LECTOR HOUSE

LECTOR HOUSE LLP
E-MAIL: info@lectorhouse.com

THE STUDY OF CELTIC LITERATURE

BY

MATTHEW ARNOLD

Popular Edition

1891

INTRODUCTION.

THE following remarks on the study of Celtic Literature formed the substance of four lectures given by me in the chair of poetry at Oxford. They were first published in the *Cornhill Magazine*, and are now reprinted from thence. Again and again, in the course of them, I have marked the very humble scope intended; which is, not to treat any special branch of scientific Celtic studies (a task for which I am quite incompetent), but to point out the many directions in which the results of those studies offer matter of general interest, and to insist on the benefit we may all derive from knowing the Celt and things Celtic more thoroughly. It was impossible, however, to avoid touching on certain points of ethnology and philology, which can be securely handled only by those who have made these sciences the object of special study. Here the mere literary critic must owe his whole safety to his tact in choosing authorities to follow, and whatever he advances must be understood as advanced with a sense of the insecurity which, after all, attaches to such a mode of proceeding, and as put forward provisionally, by way of hypothesis rather than of confident assertion.

To mark clearly to the reader both this provisional character of much which I advance, and my own sense of it, I have inserted, as a check upon some of the positions adopted in the text, notes and comments with which Lord Strangford has kindly furnished me. Lord Strangford is hardly less distinguished for knowing ethnology and languages so scientifically than for knowing so much of them; and his interest, even from the vantage-ground of his scientific knowledge, and after making all due reserves on points of scientific detail, in my treatment,—with merely the resources and point of view of a literary critic at my command,—of such a subject as the study of Celtic Literature, is the most encouraging assurance I could have received that my attempt is not altogether a vain one.

Both Lord Strangford and others whose opinion I respect have said that I am unjust in calling Mr. Nash, the acute and learned author of *Taliesin, or the Bards and Druids of Britain*, a 'Celt-hater.' 'He is a denouncer,' says Lord Strangford in a note on this expression, 'of Celtic extravagance, that is all; he is an anti-Philocelt, a very different thing from an anti-Celt, and quite indispensable in scientific inquiry. As Philoceltism has hitherto,—hitherto, remember,—meant nothing but uncritical acceptance and irrational admiration of the beloved object's sayings and doings, without reference to truth one way or the other, it is surely in the interest of science to support him in the main. In tracing the workings of old Celtic leaven in poems which embody the Celtic soul of all time in a mediæval form, I do not see that you come into any necessary opposition with him, for your concern is with the spirit, his with the substance only.' I entirely agree with almost all which Lord

Strangford here urges, and indeed, so sincere is my respect for Mr. Nash's critical discernment and learning, and so unhesitating my recognition of the usefulness, in many respects, of the work of demolition performed by him, that in originally designating him as a Celt-hater, I hastened to add, as the reader will see by referring to the passage,[1] words of explanation and apology for so calling him. But I thought then, and I think still, that Mr. Nash, in pursuing his work of demolition, too much puts out of sight the positive and constructive performance for which this work of demolition is to clear the ground. I thought then, and I think still, that in this Celtic controversy, as in other controversies, it is most desirable both to believe and to profess that the work of construction is the fruitful and important work, and that we are demolishing only to prepare for it. Mr. Nash's scepticism seems to me,—in the aspect in which his work, on the whole, shows it,—too absolute, too stationary, too much without a future; and this tends to make it, for the non-Celtic part of his readers, less fruitful than it otherwise would be, and for his Celtic readers, harsh and repellent. I have therefore suffered my remarks on Mr. Nash still to stand, though with a little modification; but I hope he will read them by the light of these explanations, and that he will believe my sense of esteem for his work to be a thousand times stronger than my sense of difference from it.

To lead towards solid ground, where the Celt may with legitimate satisfaction point to traces of the gifts and workings of his race, and where the Englishman may find himself induced to sympathise with that satisfaction and to feel an interest in it, is the design of all the considerations urged in the following essay. Kindly taking the will for the deed, a Welshman and an old acquaintance of mine, Mr. Hugh Owen, received my remarks with so much cordiality, that he asked me to come to the Eisteddfod last summer at Chester, and there to read a paper on some topic of Celtic literature or antiquities. In answer to this flattering proposal of Mr. Owen's, I wrote him a letter which appeared at the time in several newspapers, and of which the following extract preserves all that is of any importance:—

'My knowledge of Welsh matters is so utterly insignificant that it would be impertinence in me, under any circumstances, to talk about those matters to an assemblage of persons, many of whom have passed their lives in studying them.

'Your gathering acquires more interest every year. Let me venture to say that you have to avoid two dangers in order to work all the good which your friends could desire. You have to avoid the danger of giving offence to practical men by retarding the spread of the English language in the principality. I believe that to preserve and honour the Welsh language and literature is quite compatible with not thwarting or delaying for a single hour the introduction, so undeniably useful, of a knowledge of English among all classes in Wales. You have to avoid, again, the danger of alienating men of science by a blind partial, and uncritical treatment of your national antiquities. Mr. Stephens's excellent book, *The Literature of the Cymry*, shows how perfectly Welshmen can avoid this danger if they will.

'When I see the enthusiasm these Eisteddfods can awaken in your whole people, and then think of the tastes, the literature, the amusements, of our own lower and middle class, I am filled with admiration for you. It is a consoling thought,

[1] See p. 12 of the following essay.

and one which history allows us to entertain, that nations disinherited of political success may yet leave their mark on the world's progress, and contribute powerfully to the civilisation of mankind. We in England have come to that point when the continued advance and greatness of our nation is threatened by one cause, and one cause above all. Far more than by the helplessness of an aristocracy whose day is fast coming to an end, far more than by the rawness of a lower class whose day is only just beginning, we are emperilled by what I call the "Philistinism" of our middle class. On the side of beauty and taste, vulgarity; on the side of morals and feeling, coarseness; on the side of mind and spirit, unintelligence,—this is Philistinism. Now, then, is the moment for the greater delicacy and spirituality of the Celtic peoples who are blended with us, if it be but wisely directed, to make itself prized and honoured. In a certain measure the children of Taliesin and Ossian have now an opportunity for renewing the famous feat of the Greeks, and conquering their conquerors. No service England can render the Celts by giving you a share in her many good qualities, can surpass that which the Celts can at this moment render England, by communicating to us some of theirs.'

Now certainly, in that letter, written to a Welshman and on the occasion of a Welsh festival, I enlarged on the merits of the Celtic spirit and of its works, rather than on their demerits. It would have been offensive and inhuman to do otherwise. When an acquaintance asks you to write his father's epitaph, you do not generally seize that opportunity for saying that his father was blind of one eye, and had an unfortunate habit of not paying his tradesmen's bills. But the weak side of Celtism and of its Celtic glorifiers, the danger against which they have to guard, is clearly indicated in that letter; and in the remarks reprinted in this volume,—remarks which were the original cause of Mr. Owen's writing to me, and must have been fully present to his mind when he read my letter,—the shortcomings both of the Celtic race, and of the Celtic students of its literature and antiquities, are unreservedly marked, and, so far as is necessary, blamed.[2] It was, indeed, not my purpose to make blame the chief part of what I said; for the Celts, like other people, are to be meliorated rather by developing their gifts than by chastising their defects. The wise man, says Spinoza admirably, '*de humana impotentia non nisi parce loqui curabit, at largiter de humana virtute seupotentia.*' But so far as condemnation of Celtic failure was needful towards preparing the way for the growth of Celtic virtue, I used condemnation.

The *Times*, however, prefers a shorter and sharper method of dealing with the Celts, and in a couple of leading articles, having the Chester Eisteddfod and my letter to Mr. Hugh Owen for their text, it developed with great frankness, and in its usual forcible style, its own views for the amelioration of Wales and its people. *Cease to do evil, learn to do good,* was the upshot of its exhortations to the Welsh; by *evil*, the *Times* understanding all things Celtic, and by *good*, all things English. 'The Welsh language is the curse of Wales. Its prevalence, and the ignorance of English have excluded, and even now exclude the Welsh people from the civilisation of their English neighbours. An Eisteddfod is one of the most mischievous and selfish pieces of sentimentalism which could possibly be perpetrated. It is simply a

[2] See particularly pp. 4, 5, 6, of the following essay.

foolish interference with the natural progress of civilisation and prosperity. If it is desirable that the Welsh should talk English, it is monstrous folly to encourage them in a loving fondness for their old language. Not only the energy and power, but the intelligence and music of Europe have come mainly from Teutonic sources, and this glorification of everything Celtic, if it were not pedantry, would be sheer ignorance. The sooner all Welsh specialities disappear from the face of the earth the better.'

And I need hardly say, that I myself, as so often happens to me at the hands of my own countrymen, was cruelly judged by the *Times*, and most severely treated. What I said to Mr. Owen about the spread of the English language in Wales being quite compatible with preserving and honouring the Welsh language and literature, was tersely set down as 'arrant nonsense,' and I was characterised as 'a sentimentalist who talks nonsense about the children of Taliesin and Ossian, and whose dainty taste requires something more flimsy than the strong sense and sturdy morality of his fellow Englishmen.'

As I said before, I am unhappily inured to having these harsh interpretations put by my fellow Englishmen upon what I write, and I no longer cry out about it. And then, too, I have made a study of the Corinthian or leading article style, and know its exigencies, and that they are no more to be quarrelled with than the law of gravitation. So, for my part, when I read these asperities of the *Times*, my mind did not dwell very much on my own concern in them; but what I said to myself, as I put the newspaper down, was this: '*Behold England's difficulty in governing Ireland!*'

I pass by the dauntless assumption that the agricultural peasant whom we in England, without Eisteddfods, succeed in developing, is so much finer a product of civilisation than the Welsh peasant, retarded by these 'pieces of sentimentalism.' I will be content to suppose that our 'strong sense and sturdy morality' are as admirable and as universal as the *Times* pleases. But even supposing this, I will ask did any one ever hear of strong sense and sturdy morality being thrust down other people's throats in this fashion? Might not these divine English gifts, and the English language in which they are preached, have a better chance of making their way among the poor Celtic heathen, if the English apostle delivered his message a little more agreeably? There is nothing like love and admiration for bringing people to a likeness with what they love and admire; but the Englishman seems never to dream of employing these influences upon a race he wants to fuse with himself. He employs simply material interests for his work of fusion; and, beyond these, nothing except scorn and rebuke. Accordingly there is no vital union between him and the races he has annexed; and while France can truly boast of her 'magnificent unity,' a unity of spirit no less than of name between all the people who compose her, in England the Englishman proper is in union of spirit with no one except other Englishmen proper like himself. His Welsh and Irish fellow-citizens are hardly more amalgamated with him now than they were when Wales and Ireland were first conquered, and the true unity of even these small islands has yet to be achieved. When these papers of mine on the Celtic genius and literature first appeared in the *Cornhill Magazine*, they brought me, as was natural, many communications from Welshmen and Irishmen having an interest in the subject; and one could not but be painfully struck, in reading these communications, to see how profound a feeling of aversion and severance from the English they in general manifested. Who can be surprised at it, when he observes the strain of the *Times* in the articles just quoted, and remembers that this is the characteristic strain of the Englishman in commenting on whatsoever is not himself? And then, with our boundless faith in machinery, we English expect the Welshman as a matter of course to grow attached to us, because we invite him to do business with us, and let him hold any number of public meetings and publish all the newspapers he likes! When shall we learn, that what attaches people to us is the spirit we are of, and not the machinery we employ?

Last year there was a project of holding a Breton Eisteddfod at Quimper in Brittany, and the French Home Secretary, whether wishing to protect the magnificent unity of France from inroads of Bretonism, or fearing lest the design should be used in furtherance of Legitimist intrigues, or from whatever motive, issued an order which prohibited the meeting. If Mr. Walpole had issued an order prohibiting the Chester Eisteddfod, all the Englishmen from Cornwall to John o' Groat's House would have rushed to the rescue; and our strong sense and sturdy morality would never have stopped gnashing their teeth and rending their garments till the prohibition was rescinded. What a pity our strong sense and sturdy morality fail to perceive that words like those of the *Times* create a far keener sense of estrangement and dislike than acts like those of the French Minister! Acts like those of the French Minister are attributed to reasons of State, and the Government is held blameable for them, not the French people. Articles like those of the *Times* are attributed to the want of sympathy and of sweetness of disposition in the English nature, and the whole English people gets the blame of them. And deservedly; for from some such ground of want of sympathy and sweetness in the English nature, do articles like those of the *Times* come, and to some such ground do they make appeal. The sympathetic and social virtues of the French nature, on the other hand, actually repair the breaches made by oppressive deeds of the Government, and create, among populations joined with France as the Welsh and Irish are joined with England, a sense of liking and attachment towards the French people. The French Government may discourage the German language in Alsace and prohibit Eisteddfods in Brittany; but the *Journal des Débats* never treats German music and poetry as mischievous lumber, nor tells the Bretons that the sooner all Breton specialities disappear from the face of the earth the better. Accordingly, the Bretons and Alsatians have come to feel themselves a part of France, and to feel pride in bearing the French name; while the Welsh and Irish obstinately refuse to amalgamate with us, and will not admire the Englishman as he admires himself, however much the *Times* may scold them and rate them, and assure them there is nobody on earth so admirable.

And at what a moment does it assure them of this, good heavens! At a moment when the ice is breaking up in England, and we are all beginning at last to see how much real confusion and insufficiency it covered; when, whatever may be the merits,—and they are great,—of the Englishman and of his strong sense and sturdy morality, it is growing more and more evident that, if he is to endure and advance, he must transform himself, must add something to his strong sense and sturdy morality, or at least must give to these excellent gifts of his a new development. My friend Mr. Goldwin Smith says, in his eloquent way, that England is the favourite of Heaven. Far be it from me to say that England is not the favourite of Heaven; but at this moment she reminds me more of what the prophet Isaiah calls, 'a bull in a net.' She has satisfied herself in all departments with clap-trap and routine so long, and she is now so astounded at finding they will not serve her turn any longer! And this is the moment, when Englishism pure and simple, which with all its fine qualities managed always to make itself singularly unattractive, is losing that imperturbable faith in its untransformed self which at any rate made it imposing,—this is the moment when our great organ tells the Celts that everything of theirs not English is 'simply a foolish interference with the natural progress of civilisation and prosperity;' and poor Talhaiarn, venturing to remonstrate, is commanded 'to drop his outlandish title, and to refuse even to talk Welsh in Wales!'

But let us leave the dead to bury their dead, and let us who are alive go on unto perfection. Let the Celtic members of this empire consider that they too have to transform themselves; and though the summons to transform themselves he often conveyed harshly and brutally, and with the cry to root up their wheat as well as their tares, yet that is no reason why the summons should not be followed so far as their tares are concerned. Let them consider that they are inextricably bound up with us, and that, if the suggestions in the following pages have any truth, we English, alien and uncongenial to our Celtic partners as we may have hitherto shown ourselves, have notwithstanding, beyond perhaps any other nation, a thousand latent springs of possible sympathy with them. Let them consider that new ideas and forces are stirring in England, that day by day these new ideas and forces gain in power, and that almost every one of them is the friend of the Celt and not his enemy. And, whether our Celtic partners will consider this or no, at any rate let us ourselves, all of us who are proud of being the ministers of these new ideas, work incessantly to procure for them a wider and more fruitful application; and to remove the main ground of the Celt's alienation from the Englishman, by substituting, in place of that type of Englishman with whom alone the Celt has too long been familiar, a new type, more intelligent, more gracious, and more humane.

THE STUDY OF CELTIC LITERATURE

'They went forth to the war, but they always fell.'

Ossian.

Some time ago I spent some weeks at Llandudno, on the Welsh coast. The best lodging-houses at Llandudno look eastward, towards Liverpool; and from that Saxon hive swarms are incessantly issuing, crossing the bay, and taking possession of the beach and the lodging-houses. Guarded by the Great and Little Orme's Head, and alive with the Saxon invaders from Liverpool, the eastern bay is an attractive point of interest, and many visitors to Llandudno never contemplate anything else. But, putting aside the charm of the Liverpool steamboats, perhaps the view, on this side, a little dissatisfies one after a while; the horizon wants mystery, the sea wants beauty, the coast wants verdure, and has a too bare austereness and aridity. At last one turns round and looks westward. Everything is changed. Over the mouth of the Conway and its sands is the eternal softness and mild light of the west; the low line of the mystic Anglesey, and the precipitous Penmaenmawr, and the great group of Carnedd Llewelyn and Carnedd David and their brethren fading away, hill behind hill, in an aërial haze, make the horizon; between the foot of Penmaenmawr and the bending coast of Anglesey, the sea, a silver stream, disappears one knows not whither. On this side, Wales,—Wales, where the past still lives, where every place has its tradition, every name its poetry, and where the people, the genuine people, still knows this past, this tradition, this poetry, and lives with it, and clings to it; while, alas, the prosperous Saxon on the other side, the invader from Liverpool and Birkenhead, has long ago forgotten his. And the promontory where Llandudno stands is the very centre of this tradition; it is Creuddyn, *the bloody city*, where every stone has its story; there, opposite its decaying rival, Conway Castle, is Diganwy, not decaying but long since utterly decayed, some crumbling foundations on a crag top and nothing more; Diganwy, where Mael-gwyn shut up Elphin, and where Taliesin came to free him. Below, in a fold of the hill, is Llan-rhos, the church of the marsh, where the same Mael-gwyn, a British prince of real history, a bold and licentious chief, the original, it is said, of Arthur's Lancelot, shut himself up in the church to avoid the Yellow Plague, and peeped out through a hole in the door, and saw the monster and died. Behind among the woods, is Gloddaeth, *the place of feasting*, where the bards were entertained; and farther away, up the valley of the Conway towards Llanrwst, is the Lake of Ceirio-nydd and Taliesin's grave. Or, again, looking seawards and Anglesey-wards you have Pen-mon, Seiriol's isle and priory, where Mael-gwyn lies buried; you have the *Sands of Lamentation* and Llys Helig, *Heilig's Mansion*, a mansion under the waves, a sea-buried palace and realm. *Hac ibat Simois; hic est Sigeia tellus.*

As I walked up and down, looking at the waves as they washed this Sigeian land which has never had its Homer, and listening with curiosity to the strange, unfamiliar speech of its old possessors' obscure descendants,—bathing people, vegetable-sellers, and donkey-boys, who were all about me, suddenly I heard, through the stream of unknown Welsh, words, not English, indeed, but still familiar. They came from a French nursery-maid, with some children. Profoundly ignorant of her relationship, this Gaulish Celt moved among her British cousins, speaking her polite neo-Latin tongue, and full of compassionate contempt, probably, for the Welsh barbarians and their jargon. What a revolution was here! How had the star of this daughter of Gomer waxed, while the star of these Cymry, his sons, had waned! What a difference of fortune in the two, since the days when, speaking the same language, they left their common dwelling-place in the heart of Asia; since the Cimmerians of the Euxine came in upon their western kinsmen, the sons of the giant Galates; since the sisters, Gaul and Britain, cut the mistletoe in their forests, and saw the coming of Cæsar! *Blanc, rouge, rocher champ, église, seigneur*,—these words, by which the Gallo-Roman Celt now names white, and red, and rock, and field, and church, and lord, are no part of the speech of his true ancestors, they are words he has learnt; but since he learned them they have had a worldwide success, and we all teach them to our children, and armies speaking them have domineered in every city of that Germany by which the British Celt was broken, and in the train of these armies, Saxon auxiliaries, a humbled contingent, have been fain to follow; the poor Welshman still says, in the genuine tongue of his ancestors,[3] *gwyn, goch, craig, maes, llan, arglwydd*; but his land is a province, and his history petty, and his Saxon subduers scout his speech as an obstacle to civilisation; and the echo of all its kindred in other lands is growing every day fainter and more feeble; gone in Cornwall, going in Brittany and the Scotch Highlands, going, too, in Ireland; and there, above all, the badge of the beaten race, the property of

[3] Lord Strangford remarks on this passage:—'Your Gomer and your Cimmerians are of course only lay figures, to be accepted in the rhetorical and subjective sense. As such I accept them, but I enter a protest against the "genuine tongue of his ancestors." Modern Celtic tongues are to the old Celtic heard by Julius Cæsar, broadly speaking, what the modern Romanic tongues are to Cæsar's own Latin. Welsh, in fact, is a *detritus*; a language in the category of modern French, or, to speak less roughly and with a closer approximation, of old Provençal, not in the category of Lithuanian, much less in the category of Basque. By true inductive research, based on an accurate comparison of such forms of Celtic speech, oral and recorded, as we now possess, modern philology has, in so far as was possible, succeeded in restoring certain forms of the parent speech, and in so doing has achieved not the least striking of its many triumphs; for those very forms thus restored have since been verified past all cavil by their actual discovery in the old Gaulish inscriptions recently come to light. The *phonesis* of Welsh as it stands is modern, not primitive its grammar,—the verbs excepted,—is constructed out of the fragments of its earlier forms, and its vocabulary is strongly Romanised, two out of the six words here given being Latin of the Empire. Rightly understood, this enhances the value of modern Celtic instead of depreciating it, because it serves to rectify it. To me it is a wonder that Welsh should have retained so much of its integrity under the iron pressure of four hundred years of Roman dominion. Modern Welsh tenacity and cohesive power under English pressure is nothing compared with what that must have been.'

the vanquished.

But the Celtic genius was just then preparing, in Llandudno, to have its hour of revival. Workmen were busy in putting up a large tent-like wooden building, which attracted the eye of every newcomer, and which my little boys believed (their wish, no doubt, being father to their belief,) to be a circus. It turned out, however, to be no circus for Castor and Pollux, but a temple for Apollo and the Muses. It was the place where the Eisteddfod, or Bardic Congress of Wales, was about to be held; a meeting which has for its object (I quote the words of its promoters) 'the diffusion of useful knowledge, the eliciting of native talent, and the cherishing of love of home and honourable fame by the cultivation of poetry, music, and art.' My little boys were disappointed; but I, whose circus days are over, I, who have a professional interest in poetry, and who, also, hating all one-sidedness and oppression, wish nothing better than that the Celtic genius should be able to show itself to the world and to make its voice heard, was delighted. I took my ticket, and waited impatiently for the day of opening. The day came, an unfortunate one; storms of wind, clouds of dust, an angry, dirty sea. The Saxons who arrived by the Liverpool steamers looked miserable; even the Welsh who arrived by land,—whether they were discomposed by the bad morning, or by the monstrous and crushing tax which the London and North-Western Railway Company levies on all whom it transports across those four miles of marshy peninsula between Conway and Llandudno,—did not look happy. First we went to the Gorsedd, or preliminary congress for conferring the degree of bard. The Gorsedd was held in the open air, at the windy corner of a street, and the morning was not favourable to open-air solemnities. The Welsh, too, share, it seems to me, with their Saxon invaders, an inaptitude for show and spectacle. Show and spectacle are better managed by the Latin race and those whom it has moulded; the Welsh, like us, are a little awkward and resourceless in the organisation of a festival. The presiding genius of the mystic circle, in our hideous nineteenth-century costume, relieved only by a green scarf, the wind drowning his voice and the dust powdering his whiskers, looked thoroughly wretched; so did the aspirants for bardic honours; and I believe, after about an hour of it, we all of us, as we stood shivering round the sacred stones, began half to wish for the Druid's sacrificial knife to end our sufferings. But the Druid's knife is gone from his hands; so we sought the shelter of the Eisteddfod building.

The sight inside was not lively. The president and his supporters mustered strong on the platform. On the floor the one or two front benches were pretty well filled, but their occupants were for the most part Saxons, who came there from curiosity, not from enthusiasm; and all the middle and back benches, where should have been the true enthusiasts,—the Welsh people, were nearly empty. The president, I am sure, showed a national spirit which was admirable. He addressed us Saxons in our own language, and called us 'the English branch of the descendants of the ancient Britons.' We received the compliment with the impassive dulness which is the characteristic of our nature; and the lively Celtic nature, which should have made up for the dulness of ours, was absent. A lady who sat by me, and who was the wife, I found, of a distinguished bard on the platform, told me, with emotion in her look and voice, how dear were these solemnities to the heart of her people, how deep was the interest which is aroused by them. I believe her, but still the whole performance, on that particular morning, was incurably lifeless. The recitation of the prize compositions began: pieces of verse and prose in the Welsh language, an essay on punctuality being, if I remember right, one of them; a poem on the march of Havelock, another. This went on for some time. Then Dr. Vaughan,—the well-known Nonconformist minister, a Welshman, and a good patriot,—addressed us in English. His speech was a powerful one, and he succeeded, I confess, in sending a faint thrill through our front benches; but it was the old familiar thrill which we have all of us felt a thousand times in Saxon chapels and meeting-halls, and had nothing bardic about it. I stepped out, and in the street I came across an acquaintance fresh from London and the parliamentary session. In a moment the spell of the Celtic genius was forgotten, the Philistinism of our Saxon nature made itself felt; and my friend and I walked up and down by the roaring waves, talking not of ovates and bards, and triads and englyns, but of the sewage question, and the glories of our local self-government, and the mysterious perfections of the Metropolitan Board of Works.

I believe it is admitted, even by the admirers of Eisteddfods in general, that this particular Eisteddfod was not a success. Llandudno, it is said, was not the right place for it. Held in Conway Castle, as a few years ago it was, and its spectators,—an enthusiastic multitude,—filling the grand old ruin, I can imagine it a most impressive and interesting sight, even to a stranger labouring under the terrible disadvantage of being ignorant of the Welsh language. But even seen as I saw it at Llandudno, it had the power to set one thinking. An Eisteddfod is, no doubt, a kind of Olympic meeting; and that the common people of Wales should care for such a thing, shows something Greek in them, something spiritual, something humane, something (I am afraid one must add) which in the English common people is not to be found. This line of reflection has been followed by the accomplished Bishop of St. David's, and by the *Saturday Review*, it is just, it is fruitful, and those who pursued it merit our best thanks. But, from peculiar circumstances, the Llandudno meeting was, as I have said, such as not at all to suggest ideas of Olympia, and of a multitude touched by the divine flame, and hanging on the lips of Pindar. It rather suggested the triumph of the prosaic, practical Saxon, and the approaching extinction of an enthusiasm which he derides as factitious, a literature which he disdains as trash, a language which he detests as a nuisance.

I must say I quite share the opinion of my brother Saxons as to the practical inconvenience of perpetuating the speaking of Welsh. It may cause a moment's distress to one's imagination when one hears that the last Cornish peasant who spoke the old tongue of Cornwall is dead; but, no doubt, Cornwall is the better for adopting English, for becoming more thoroughly one with the rest of the country. The fusion of all the inhabitants of these islands into one homogeneous, English-speaking whole, the breaking down of barriers between us, the swallowing up of separate provincial nationalities, is a consummation to which the natural course of things irresistibly tends; it is a necessity of what is called modern civilisation, and modern civilisation is a real, legitimate force; the change must come, and its accomplishment is a mere affair of time. The sooner the Welsh language disappears as an instrument of the practical, political, social life of Wales, the better; the better for England, the better for Wales itself. Traders and tourists do excellent service by pushing the English wedge farther and farther into the heart of the principality; Ministers of Education, by hammering it harder and harder into the elementary schools. Nor, perhaps, can one have much sympathy with the literary cultivation of Welsh as an instrument of living literature; and in this respect Eisteddfods encourage, I think, a fantastic and mischief-working delusion.

For all serious purposes in modern literature (and trifling purposes in it who would care to encourage?) the language of a Welshman is and must be English; if an Eisteddfod author has anything to say about punctuality or about the march of Havelock, he had much better say it in English; or rather, perhaps, what he has to say on these subjects may as well be said in Welsh, but the moment he has anything of real importance to say, anything the world will the least care to hear, he must speak English. Dilettanteism might possibly do much harm here, might mislead and waste and bring to nought a genuine talent. For all modern purposes, I repeat, let us all as soon as possible be one people; let the Welshman speak English, and, if he is an author, let him write English.

So far, I go along with the stream of my brother Saxons; but here, I imagine, I part company with them. They will have nothing to do with the Welsh language and literature on any terms; they would gladly make a clean sweep of it from the face of the earth. I, on certain terms, wish to make a great deal more of it than is made now; and I regard the Welsh literature,—or rather, dropping the distinction between Welsh and Irish, Gaels and Cymris, let me say Celtic literature,—as an object of very great interest. My brother Saxons have, as is well known, a terrible way with them of wanting to improve everything but themselves off the face of the earth; I have no such passion for finding nothing but myself everywhere; I like variety to exist and to show itself to me, and I would not for the world have the lineaments of the Celtic genius lost. But I know my brother Saxons, I know their strength, and I know that the Celtic genius will make nothing of trying to set up barriers against them in the world of fact and brute force, of trying to hold its own against them as a political and social counter-power, as the soul of a hostile nationality. To me there is something mournful (and at this moment, when one sees what is going on in Ireland, how well may one say so!) in hearing a Welshman or an Irishman make pretensions,—natural pretensions, I admit, but how hopelessly vain!—to such a rival self-establishment; there is something mournful in hearing an Englishman scout them. Strength! alas, it is not strength, strength in the material world, which is wanting to us Saxons; we have plenty of strength for swallowing up and absorbing as much as we choose; there is nothing to hinder us from effacing the last poor material remains of that Celtic power which once was everywhere, but has long since, in the race of civilisation, fallen out of sight. We may threaten them with extinction if we will, and may almost say in so threatening them, like Cæsar in threatening with death the tribune Metellus who closed the treasury doors against him: 'And when I threaten this, young man, to threaten it is more trouble to me than to do it.' It is not in the outward and visible world of material life, that the Celtic genius of Wales or Ireland can at this day hope to count for much; it is in the inward world of thought and science. What it *has* been, what it *has* done, let it ask us to attend to that, as a matter of science and history; not to what it will be or will do, as a matter of modern politics. It cannot count appreciably now as a material power; but, perhaps, if it can get itself thoroughly known as an object of science, it may count for a good deal,—far more than we Saxons, most of us, imagine,—as a spiritual power.

The bent of our time is towards science, towards knowing things as they are; so the Celt's claims towards having his genius and its works fairly treated, as objects of scientific investigation, the Saxon can hardly reject, when these claims are urged simply on their own merits, and are not mixed up with extraneous pretensions which jeopardise them. What the French call the *science des origines*, the science of origins,—a science which is at the bottom of all real knowledge of the actual world, and which is every day growing in interest and importance—is very incomplete without a thorough critical account of the Celts, and their genius, language, and literature. This science has still great progress to make, but its progress, made even within the recollection of those of us who are in middle life, has already affected our common notions about the Celtic race; and this change, too, shows how science, the knowing things as they are, may even have salutary practical consequences. I remember, when I was young, I was taught to think of Celt as separated by an impassable gulf from Teuton;[4] my father, in particular, was never weary of

[4] Here again let me have the pleasure of quoting Lord Strangford:—'When the Celtic tongues were first taken in hand at the dawn of comparative philological inquiry, the tendency was, for all practical results, to separate them from the Indo-European aggregate, rather than to unite them with it. The great gulf once fixed between them was narrowed on the surface, but it was greatly and indefinitely deepened. Their vocabulary and some of their grammar were seen at once to be perfectly Indo-European, but they had no case-endings to their nouns, none at all in Welsh, none that could be understood in Gaelic; their *phonesis* seemed primeval and inexplicable, and nothing could be made out of their pronouns which could not be equally made out of many wholly un-Aryan languages. They were therefore co-ordinated, not with each single Aryan tongue, but with the general complex of Aryan tongues, and were conceived to be anterior to them and apart from them, as it were the strayed vanguard of European colonisation or conquest from the East. The reason of this misconception was, that their records lay wholly uninvestigated as far as all historical study of the language was concerned, and that nobody troubled himself about the relative age and the development of forms, so that the philologists were fain to take them as they were put into their hands by uncritical or perverse native commentators and writers, whose grammars and dictionaries teemed with blunders and downright forgeries. One thing, and one thing alone, led to the truth: the sheer drudgery of thirteen long years spent by Zeuss in the patient investigation of the most ancient Celtic records, in their actual condition, line by line and letter by letter. Then for the first time the foundation of Celtic research was laid; but the great philologist did not live to see the superstructure which never could have been raised but for him. Prichard was first to indicate the right path, and Bopp, in his monograph of 1839, displayed his incomparable and masterly sagacity as usual, but for want of any trustworthy record of Celtic words and forms to work upon, the truth remained concealed or obscured until the publication of the *Gramatica Celtica*. Dr. Arnold, a man of the past generation, who made more use of the then uncertain and unfixed doctrines of comparative philology in his historical writings than is done by the present generation in the fullest noonday light of the *Vergleichende Grammatik*, was thus justified in his view by

contrasting them; he insisted much oftener on the separation between us and them than on the separation between us and any other race in the world; in the same way Lord Lyndhurst, in words long famous, called the Irish 'aliens in speech, in religion, in blood.' This naturally created a profound sense of estrangement; it doubled the estrangement which political and religious differences already made between us and the Irish: it seemed to make this estrangement immense, incurable, fatal. It begot a strange reluctance, as any one may see by reading the preface to the great text-book for Welsh poetry, the *Myvyrian Archæology*, published at the beginning of this century, to further,—nay, allow,—even among quiet, peaceable people like the Welsh, the publication of the documents of their ancient literature, the monuments of the Cymric genius; such was the sense of repulsion, the sense of incompatibilty, of radical antagonism, making it seem dangerous to us to let such opposites to ourselves have speech and utterance. Certainly the Jew,—the Jew of ancient times, at least,—then seemed a thousand degrees nearer than the Celt to us. Puritanism had so assimilated Bible ideas and phraseology; names like Ebenezer, and notions like that of hewing Agag in pieces, came so natural to us, that the sense of affinity between the Teutonic and the Hebrew nature was quite strong; a steady, middleclass Anglo-Saxon much more imagined himself Ehud's cousin than Ossian's. But meanwhile, the pregnant and striking ideas of the ethnologists about the true natural grouping of the human race, the doctrine of a great Indo-European unity, comprising Hindoos, Persians, Greeks, Latins, Celts, Teutons, Slavonians, on the one hand, and, on the other hand, of a Semitic unity and of a Mongolian unity, separated by profound distinguishing marks from the Indo-European unity and from one another, was slowly acquiring consistency and popularising itself. So strong and real could the sense of sympathy or antipathy, grounded upon real identity or diversity in race, grow in men of culture, that we read of a genuine Teuton,—Wilhelm von Humboldt—finding, even in the sphere of religion, that sphere where the might of Semitism has been so overpowering, the food which most truly suited his spirit in the productions not of the alien Semitic genius, but of the genius of Greece or India, the Teutons born kinsfolk of the common Indo-European family. 'Towards Semitism he felt himself,' we read, 'far less drawn;' he had the consciousness of a certain antipathy in the depths of his nature to this, and to its 'absorbing, tyrannous, terrorist religion,' as to the opener, more flexible Indo-European genius, this religion appeared. 'The mere workings of the old man in him!' Semitism will readily reply; and though one can hardly admit this short and easy method of settling the matter, it must be owned that Humboldt's is an extreme case of Indo-Europeanism, useful as letting us see what may be the power of race and primitive constitution, but not likely, in the spiritual sphere, to have many companion cases equalling it. Still, even in this sphere, the tendency is in Humboldt's direction; the modern spirit tends more and more to establish a sense of native diversity between our European bent and the Semitic and to eliminate, even in our religion, certain elements as purely and excessively Semitic, and therefore, in right, not combinable with our European nature, not

the philology of the period, to which he merely gave an enlarged historical expression. The prime fallacy then as now, however, was that of antedating the distinction between Gaelic and Cymric Celts.'

assimilable by it. This tendency is now quite visible even among ourselves, and even, as I have said, within the great sphere of the Semitic genius, the sphere of religion; and for its justification this tendency appeals to science, the science of origins; it appeals to this science as teaching us which way our natural affinities and repulsions lie. It appeals to this science, and in part it comes from it; it is, in considerable part, an indirect practical result from it.

In the sphere of politics, too, there has, in the same way, appeared an indirect practical result from this science; the sense of antipathy to the Irish people, of radical estrangement from them, has visibly abated amongst all the better part of us; the remorse for past ill-treatment of them, the wish to make amends, to do them justice, to fairly unite, if possible, in one people with them, has visibly increased; hardly a book on Ireland is now published, hardly a debate on Ireland now passes in Parliament, without this appearing. Fanciful as the notion may at first seem, I am inclined to think that the march of science,—science insisting that there is no such original chasm between the Celt and the Saxon as we once popularly imagined, that they are not truly, what Lord Lyndhurst called them, *aliens in blood* from us, that they are our brothers in the great Indo-European family,—has had a share, an appreciable share, in producing this changed state of feeling. No doubt, the release from alarm and struggle, the sense of firm possession, solid security, and overwhelming power; no doubt these, allowing and encouraging humane feelings to spring up in us, have done much; no doubt a state of fear and danger, Ireland in hostile conflict with us, our union violently disturbed, might, while it drove back all humane feelings, make also the old sense of utter estrangement revive. Nevertheless, so long as such a malignant revolution of events does not actually come about, so long the new sense of kinship and kindliness lives, works, and gathers strength; and the longer it so lives and works, the more it makes any such malignant revolution improbable. And this new, reconciling sense has, I say, its roots in science.

However, on these indirect benefits of science we must not lay too much stress. Only this must be allowed; it is clear that there are now in operation two influences, both favourable to a more attentive and impartial study of Celtism than it has yet ever received from us. One is, the strengthening in us of the feeling of Indo-Europeanism; the other, the strengthening in us of the scientific sense generally. The first breaks down barriers between us and the Celt, relaxes the estrangement between us; the second begets the desire to know his case thoroughly, and to be just to it. This is a very different matter from the political and social Celtisation of which certain enthusiasts dream; but it is not to be despised by any one to whom the Celtic genius is dear; and it is possible, while the other is not.

I.

To know the Celtic case thoroughly, one must know the Celtic people; and to know them, one must know that by which a people best express themselves,—their literature. Few of us have any notion what a mass of Celtic literature is really yet extant and accessible. One constantly finds even very accomplished people, who fancy that the remains of Welsh and Irish literature are as inconsiderable by their volume, as, in their opinion, they are by their intrinsic merit; that these remains consist of a few prose stories, in great part borrowed from the literature of nations more civilised than the Welsh or Irish nation, and of some unintelligible poetry. As to Welsh literature, they have heard, perhaps, of the *Black Book of Caermarthen*, or of the *Red Book of Hergest*, and they imagine that one or two famous manuscript books like these contain the whole matter. They have no notion that, in real truth, to quote the words of one who is no friend to the high pretensions of Welsh literature, but their most formidable impugner, Mr. Nash:—'The Myvyrian manuscripts alone, now deposited in the British Museum, amount to 47 volumes of poetry, of various sizes, containing about 4,700 pieces of poetry, in 16,000 pages, besides about 2,000 englynion or epigrammatic stanzas. There are also, in the same collection, 53 volumes of prose, in about 15,300 pages, containing great many curious documents on various subjects. Besides these, which were purchased of the widow of the celebrated Owen Jones, the editor of the *Myvyrian Archæology*, there are a vast number of collections of Welsh manuscripts in London, and in the libraries of the gentry of the principality.' The *Myvyrian Archæology*, here spoken of by Mr. Nash, I have already mentioned; he calls its editor, Owen Jones, celebrated; he is not so celebrated but that he claims a word, in passing, from a professor of poetry. He was a Denbighshire *statesman*, as we say in the north, born before the middle of last century, in that vale of Myvyr, which has given its name to his archæology. From his childhood he had that passion for the old treasures of his Country's literature, which to this day, as I have said, in the common people of Wales is so remarkable; these treasures were unprinted, scattered, difficult of access, jealously guarded. 'More than once,' says Edward Lhuyd, who in his *Archæologia Britannica*, brought out by him in 1707, would gladly have given them to the world, 'more than once I had a promise from the owner, and the promise was afterwards retracted at the instigation of certain persons, pseudo-politicians, as I think, rather than men of letters.' So Owen Jones went up, a young man of nineteen, to London, and got employment in a furrier's shop in Thames Street; for forty years, with a single object in view, he worked at his business; and at the end of that time his object was won. He had risen in his employment till the business had become his own, and he was now a man of considerable means; but those means had been sought by him for one purpose only, the purpose of his life, the dream of his youth,—the giving permanence and publicity to the treasures of his national literature. Gradually he got manuscript after manuscript transcribed, and at last, in 1801, he jointly with two friends brought out in three large volumes, printed in double columns, his *Myvyrian Archæology of Wales*. The book is full of imperfections, it presented itself to a public which could not judge of its importance, and it brought upon its author, in his lifetime, more attack than honour. He died not long afterwards, and now he lies buried in Allhallows Church, in London, with his tomb turned towards the east, away from the green vale of Clwyd and the mountains of his native Wales; but his book is the great repertory of the literature of his nation, the comparative study of languages and literatures gains every day more followers, and no one of these followers, at home or abroad, touches Welsh literature without paying homage to the Denbighshire peasant's name; if the bard's glory and his own are still matter of moment to him,—*si quid mentem mortalia tangunt*,—he may be satisfied.

Even the printed stock of early Welsh literature is, therefore, considerable, and the manuscript stock of it is very great indeed. Of Irish literature, the stock, printed and manuscript, is truly vast; the work of cataloguing and describing this has been admirably performed by another remarkable man, who died only the other day, Mr. Eugene O'Curry. Obscure Scaliger of a despised literature, he deserves some weightier voice to praise him than the voice of an unlearned bellettristic trifler like me; he belongs to the race of the giants in literary research and industry,—a race now almost extinct. Without a literary education, and impeded too, it appears, by much trouble of mind and infirmity of body, he has accomplished such a thorough work of classification and description for the chaotic mass of Irish literature, that the student has now half his labour saved, and needs only to use his materials as Eugene O'Curry hands them to him. It was as a professor in the Catholic University in Dublin that O'Curry gave the lectures in which he has done the student this service; it is touching to find that these lectures, a splendid tribute of devotion to the Celtic cause, had no hearer more attentive, more sympathising, than a man, himself, too, the champion of a cause more interesting than prosperous,—one of those causes which please noble spirits, but do not please destiny, which have Cato's adherence, but not Heaven's,—Dr. Newman. Eugene O'Curry, in these lectures of his, taking as his standard the quarto page of Dr. O'Donovan's edition of the *Annals of the Four Masters* (and this printed monument of one branch of Irish literature occupies by itself, let me say in passing, seven large quarto volumes, containing 4,215 pages of closely printed matter), Eugene O'Curry says, that the great vellum manuscript books belonging to Trinity College, Dublin, and to the Royal Irish Academy,—books with fascinating titles, the *Book of the Dun Cow*, the *Book of Leinster*, the *Book of Ballymote*, the *Speckled Book*, the *Book of Lecain*, the *Yellow Book of Lecain*,—have, between them, matter enough to fill 11,400 of these pages; the other vellum manuscripts in the library of Trinity College, Dublin, have matter enough to fill 8,200 pages more; and the paper manuscripts of Trinity College, and the Royal Irish Academy together, would fill, he says, 30,000 such pages more. The ancient laws of Ireland, the so-called Brehon laws, which a commission is now publishing, were not as yet completely transcribed when O'Curry wrote; but what had even then been transcribed was sufficient, he says, to fill nearly 8,000 of Dr. O'Donovan's pages. Here are, at any rate, materials enough with a vengeance. These materials fall, of course, into several divisions. The most literary of these divisions, the *Tales*, consisting of *Historic Tales* and *Imaginative Tales*, distributes the contents of its *Historic Tales* as follows:—Battles, voyages, sieges, tragedies, cow-spoils, courtships, adventures, land-expeditions, sea-expeditions, banquets, elopements, loves, lake-irruptions, colonisations, visions. Of what a treasure-house of resources for the history of Celtic life and the Celtic genius does that bare list, even by itself, call up the image! The *Annals of the Four Masters* give 'the years of foundations and destructions of churches and castles, the obituaries of remarkable persons, the inaugurations of kings, the battles of chiefs, the contests of clans, the ages of bards, abbots, bishops, &c.'[5] Through other divisions of this mass of materials,—the books of pedigrees and genealogies, the martyrologies and festologies, such as the *Féliré of Angus the Culdee*, the topographical tracts, such as the

[5] Dr. O'Conor in his *Catalogue of the Stowe MSS.* (quoted by O'Curry).

Dinnsenchas,—we touch 'the most ancient traditions of the Irish, traditions which were committed to writing at a period when the ancient customs of the people were unbroken.' We touch 'the early history of Ireland, civil and ecclesiastical.' We get 'the origin and history of the countless monuments of Ireland, of the ruined church and tower, the sculptured cross, the holy well, and the commemorative name of almost every townland and parish in the whole island.' We get, in short, 'the most detailed information upon almost every part of ancient Gaelic life, a vast quantity of valuable details of life and manners.'[6]

And then, besides, to our knowledge of the Celtic genius, Mr. Norris has brought us from Cornwall, M. de la Villemarqué from Brittany, contributions, insignificant indeed in quantity, if one compares them with the mass of the Irish materials extant, but far from insignificant in value.

We want to know what all this mass of documents really tells us about the Celt. But the mode of dealing with these documents, and with the whole question of Celtic antiquity, has hitherto been most unsatisfactory. Those who have dealt with them, have gone to work, in general, either as warm Celt-lovers or as warm Celt-haters, and not as disinterested students of an important matter of science. One party seems to set out with the determination to find everything in Celtism and its remains; the other, with the determination to find nothing in them. A simple seeker for truth has a hard time between the two. An illustration or so will make clear what I mean. First let us take the Celt-lovers, who, though they engage one's sympathies more than the Celt-haters, yet, inasmuch as assertion is more dangerous than denial, show their weaknesses in a more signal way. A very learned man, the Rev. Edward Davies, published in the early part of this century two important books on Celtic antiquity. The second of these books, *The Mythology and Rites of the British Druids*, contains, with much other interesting matter, the charming story of Taliesin. Bryant's book on mythology was then in vogue, and Bryant, in the fantastical manner so common in those days, found in Greek mythology what he called an arkite idolatry, pointing to Noah's deluge and the ark. Davies, wishing to give dignity to his Celtic mythology, determines to find the arkite idolatry there too, and the style in which he proceeds to do this affords a good specimen of the extravagance which has caused Celtic antiquity to be looked upon with so much suspicion. The story of Taliesin begins thus:—

'In former times there was a man of noble descent in Penllyn. His name was Tegid Voel, and his paternal estate was in the middle of the Lake of Tegid, and his wife was called Ceridwen.'

Nothing could well be simpler; but what Davies finds in this simple opening of Taliesin's story is prodigious:—

'Let us take a brief view of the proprietor of this estate. Tegid Voel—*bald serenity*—presents itself at once to our fancy. The painter would find no embarrassment in sketching the portrait of this sedate venerable personage, whose crown is partly stripped of its hoary honours. But of all the gods of antiquity, none could with propriety sit for this picture excepting Saturn, the acknowledged representative

[6] O'Curry.

of Noah, and the husband of Rhea, which was but another name for Ceres, the genius of the ark.'

And Ceres, the genius of the ark, is of course found in Ceridwen, 'the British Ceres, the arkite goddess who initiates us into the deepest mysteries of the arkite superstition.'

Now the story of Taliesin, as it proceeds, exhibits Ceridwen as a sorceress; and a sorceress, like a goddess, belongs to the world of the supernatural; but, beyond this, the story itself does not suggest one particle of relationship between Ceridwen and Ceres. All the rest comes out of Davies's fancy, and is established by reasoning of the force of that about 'bald serenity.'

It is not difficult for the other side, the Celt-haters, to get a triumph over such adversaries as these. Perhaps I ought to ask pardon of Mr. Nash, whose *Taliesin* it is impossible to read without profit and instruction, for classing him among the Celt-haters; his determined scepticism about Welsh antiquity seems to me, however, to betray a preconceived hostility, a bias taken beforehand, as unmistakable as Mr. Davies's prepossessions. But Mr. Nash is often very happy in demolishing, for really the Celt-lovers seem often to try to lay themselves open, and to invite demolition. Full of his notions about an arkite idolatry and a Helio-dæmonic worship, Edward Davies gives this translation of an old Welsh poem, entitled *The Panegyric of Lludd the Great*:—

'A song of dark import was composed by the distinguished Ogdoad, who assembled on the day of the moon, and went in open procession. On the day of Mars they allotted wrath to their adversaries; and on the day of Mercury they enjoyed their full pomp; on the day of Jove they were delivered from the detested usurpers; on the day of Venus, the day of the great influx, they swam in the blood of men;[7] on the day of the Sun there truly assemble five ships and five hundred of those who make supplication: O Brithi, O Brithoi! O son of the compacted wood, the shock overtakes me; we all attend on Adonai, on the area of Pwmpai.'

That looks Helio-dæmonic enough, undoubtedly; especially when Davies prints *O Brithi, O Brithoi*! in Hebrew characters, as being 'vestiges of sacred hymns in the Phœnician language.' But then comes Mr. Nash, and says that the poem is a middle-age composition, with nothing Helio-dæmonic about it; that it is meant to ridicule the monks; and that *O Brithi, O Brithoi*! is a mere piece of unintelligible jargon in mockery of the chants used by the monks at prayers; and he gives this counter-translation of the poem:—

'They make harsh songs; they note eight numbers. On Monday they will be prying about. On Tuesday they separate, angry with their adversaries. On Wednesday they drink, enjoying themselves ostentatiously. On Thursday they are in the choir; their poverty is disagreeable. Friday is a day of abundance, the men are swimming in pleasures. On Sunday, certainly, five legions and five hundreds of them, they pray, they make exclamations: O Brithi, O Brithoi! Like wood-cuckoos in noise they will be, every one of the idiots banging on the ground.'

As one reads Mr. Nash's explanation and translation after Edward Davies's,

[7] Here, where Saturday should come, something is wanting in the manuscript.

one feels that a flood of the broad daylight of common-sense has been suddenly shed over the *Panegyric on Lludd the Great*, and one is very grateful to Mr. Nash.

Or, again, when another Celt-lover, Mr. Herbert, has bewildered us with his fancies, as uncritical as Edward Davies's; with his neo-Druidism, his Mithriac heresy, his Crist-celi, or man-god of the mysteries; and above all, his ape of the sanctuary, 'signifying the mercurial principle, that strange and unexplained disgrace of paganism,' Mr. Nash comes to our assistance, and is most refreshingly rational. To confine ourselves to the ape of the sanctuary only. Mr. Herbert constructs his monster,—to whom, he says, 'great sanctity, together with foul crime, deception, and treachery,' is ascribed,—out of four lines of old Welsh poetry, of which he adopts the following translation:—

'Without the ape, without the stall of the cow, without the mundane rampart, the world will become desolate, not requiring the cuckoos to convene the appointed dance over the green.'

One is not very clear what all this means, but it has, at any rate, a solemn air about it, which prepares one for the development of its first-named personage, the ape, into the mystical ape of the sanctuary. The cow, too,—says another famous Celt-lover, Dr. Owen, the learned author of the Welsh Dictionary,—the cow (*henfon*) is the cow of transmigration; and this also sounds natural enough. But Mr. Nash, who has a keen eye for the piecing which frequently happens in these old fragments, has observed that just here, where the ape of the sanctuary and the cow of transmigration make their appearance, there seems to come a cluster of adages, popular sayings; and he at once remembers an adage preserved with the word *henfon* in it, where, as he justly says, 'the cow of transmigration cannot very well have place.' This adage, rendered literally in English, is: 'Whoso owns the old cow, let him go at her tail;' and the meaning of it, as a popular saying, is clear and simple enough. With this clue, Mr. Nash examines the whole passage, suggests that *heb eppa*, 'without the ape,' with which Mr. Herbert begins, in truth belongs to something going before and is to be translated somewhat differently; and, in short, that what we really have here is simply these three adages one after another: 'The first share is the full one. Politeness is natural, says the ape. Without the cow-stall there would be no dung-heap.' And one can hardly doubt that Mr. Nash is quite right.

Even friends of the Celt, who are perfectly incapable of extravagances of this sort, fall too often into a loose mode of criticism concerning him and the documents of his history, which is unsatisfactory in itself, and also gives an advantage to his many enemies. One of the best and most delightful friends he has ever had,—M. de la Villemarqué,—has seen clearly enough that often the alleged antiquity of his documents cannot be proved, that it can be even disproved, and that he must rely on other supports than this to establish what he wants; yet one finds him saying: 'I open the collection of Welsh bards from the sixth to the tenth century. Taliesin, one of the oldest of them,' . . . and so on. But his adversaries deny that we have really any such thing as a 'collection of Welsh bards from the sixth to the tenth century,' or that a 'Taliesin, one of the oldest of them,' exists to be quoted in defence of any thesis. Sharon Turner, again, whose *Vindication of the Ancient British*

Poems was prompted, it seems to me, by a critical instinct at bottom sound, is weak and uncritical in details like this: 'The strange poem of Taliesin, called the *Spoils of Annwn,* implies the existence (in the sixth century, he means) of mythological tales about Arthur; and the frequent allusion of the old Welsh bards to the persons and incidents which we find in the *Mabinogion,* are further proofs that there must have been such stories in circulation amongst the Welsh.' But the critic has to show, against his adversaries, that the *Spoils of Annwn* is a real poem of the sixth century, with a real sixth-century poet called Taliesin for its author, before he can use it to prove what Sharon Turner there wishes to prove; and, in like manner, the high antiquity of persons and incidents that are found in the manuscripts of the *Mabinogion,*—manuscripts written, like the famous *Red Book of Hergest,* in the library of Jesus College at Oxford, in the fourteenth and fifteenth centuries,—is not proved by allusions of the old Welsh bards, until (which is just the question at issue) the pieces containing these allusions are proved themselves to possess a very high antiquity. In the present state of the question as to the early Welsh literature, this sort of reasoning is inconclusive and bewildering, and merely carries us round in a circle. Again, it is worse than inconclusive reasoning, it shows so uncritical a spirit that it begets grave mistrust, when Mr. Williams ab Ithel, employed by the Master of the Rolls to edit the *Brut y Tywysogion,* the 'Chronicle of the Princes,' says in his introduction, in many respects so useful and interesting: 'We may add, on the authority of a scrupulously faithful antiquary, and one that was deeply versed in the traditions of his order—the late Iolo Morganwg—that King Arthur in his Institutes of the Round Table introduced the age of the world for events which occurred before Christ, and the year of Christ's nativity for all subsequent events.' Now, putting out of the question Iolo Morganwg's character as an antiquary, it is obvious that no one, not Grimm himself, can stand in that way as 'authority' for King Arthur's having thus regulated chronology by his Institutes of the Round Table, or even for there ever having been any such institutes at all. And finally, greatly as I respect and admire Mr. Eugene O'Curry, unquestionable as is the sagacity, the moderation, which he in general unites with his immense learning, I must say that he, too, like his brother Celt-lovers, sometimes lays himself dangerously open. For instance, the Royal Irish Academy possesses in its Museum a relic of the greatest value, the *Domhnach Airgid,* a Latin manuscript of the four gospels. The outer box containing this manuscript is of the fourteenth century, but the manuscript itself, says O'Curry (and no man is better able to judge) is certainly of the sixth. This is all very well. 'But,' O'Curry then goes on, 'I believe no reasonable doubt can exist that the *Domhnach Airgid* was actually sanctified by the hand of our great Apostle.' One has a thrill of excitement at receiving this assurance from such a man as Eugene O'Curry; one believes that he is really going to make it clear that St. Patrick did actually sanctify the *Domhnach Airgid* with his own hands; and one reads on:—

'As St. Patrick, says an ancient life of St. Mac Carthainn preserved by Colgan in his *Acta Sanctorum Hiberniæ,* was on his way from the north, and coming to the place now called Clogher, he was carried over a stream by his strong man, Bishop Mac Carthainn, who, while bearing the Saint, groaned aloud, exclaiming: "Ugh! Ugh!"

'"Upon my good word," said the Saint, "it was not usual with you to make that noise."

'"I am now old and infirm," said Bishop Mac Carthainn, "and all my early companions in mission-work you have settled down in their respective churches, while I am still on my travels."

'"Found a church then," said the Saint, "that shall not be too near us" (that is to his own Church of Armagh) "for familiarity, nor too far from us for intercourse."

'And the Saint then left Bishop Mac Carthainn there, at Clogher, and bestowed the *Domhnach Airgid* upon him, which had been given to Patrick from heaven, when he was on the sea, coming to Erin.'

The legend is full of poetry, full of humour; and one can quite appreciate, after reading it, the tact which gave St. Patrick such a prodigious success in organising the primitive church in Ireland; the new bishop, 'not too near us for familiarity, nor too far from us for intercourse,' is a masterpiece. But how can Eugene O'Curry have imagined that it takes no more than a legend like that, to prove that the particular manuscript now in the Museum of the Royal Irish Academy was once in St. Patrick's pocket?

I insist upon extravagances like these, not in order to throw ridicule upon the Celt-lovers,—on the contrary, I feel a great deal of sympathy with them,—but rather, to make it clear what an immense advantage the Celt-haters, the negative side, have in the controversy about Celtic antiquity; how much a clear-headed sceptic, like Mr. Nash, may utterly demolish, and, in demolishing, give himself the appearance of having won an entire victory. But an entire victory he has, as I will next proceed to show, by no means won.

II.

I said that a sceptic like Mr. Nash, by demolishing the rubbish of the Celtic antiquaries, might often give himself the appearance of having won a complete victory, but that a complete victory he had, in truth, by no means won. He has cleared much rubbish away, but this is no such very difficult feat, and requires mainly common-sense; to be sure, Welsh archæologists are apt to lose their common-sense, but at moments when they are in possession of it they can do the indispensable, negative part of criticism, not, indeed, so briskly or cleverly as Mr. Nash, but still well enough. Edward Davies, for instance, has quite clearly seen that the alleged remains of old Welsh literature are not to be taken for genuine just as they stand: 'Some petty and mendicant minstrel, who only chaunted it as an old song, has tacked on' (he says of a poem he is discussing) 'these lines, in a style and measure totally different from the preceding verses: "May the Trinity grant us mercy in the day of judgment: a liberal donation, good gentlemen!"' There, fifty years before Mr. Nash, is a clearance like one of Mr. Nash's. But the difficult feat in this matter is the feat of construction; to determine when one has cleared away all that is to be cleared away, what is the significance of that which is left; and here, I confess, I think Mr. Nash and his fellow-sceptics, who say that next to nothing is left, and that the significance of whatever is left is next to nothing, dissatisfy the genuine critic even more than Edward Davies and his brother enthusiasts, who have a sense that something primitive, august, and interesting is there, though they fail to extract it, dissatisfy him. There is a very edifying story told by O'Curry of the effect produced on Moore, the poet, who had undertaken to write the history of Ireland (a task for which he was quite unfit), by the contemplation of an old Irish manuscript. Moore had, without knowing anything about them, spoken slightingly of the value to the historian of Ireland of the materials afforded by such manuscripts; but, says O'Curry:—

'In the year 1839, during one of his last visits to the land of his birth, he, in company with his old and attached friend Dr. Petrie, favoured me with an unexpected visit at the Royal Irish Academy. I was at that period employed on the Ordnance Survey of Ireland, and at the time of his visit happened to have before me on my desk the *Books of Ballymote and Lecain, The Speckled Book, The Annals of the Four Masters*, and many other ancient books, for historical research and reference. I had never before seen Moore, and after a brief introduction and explanation of the nature of my occupation by Dr. Petrie, and seeing the formidable array of so many dark and time-worn volumes by which I was surrounded, he looked a little disconcerted, but after a while plucked up courage to open the *Book of Ballymote* and ask what it was. Dr. Petrie and myself then entered into a short explanation of the history and character of the books then present as well as of ancient Gaedhelic documents in general. Moore listened with great attention, alternately scanning the books and myself, and then asked me, in a serious tone, if I understood them, and how I had learned to do so. Having satisfied him upon these points, he turned to Dr. Petrie and said:—"Petrie, these huge tomes could not have been written by fools or for any foolish purpose. I never knew anything about them before, and I had no right to have undertaken the History of Ireland."'

And from that day Moore, it is said, lost all heart for going on with his *History of Ireland*, and it was only the importunity of the publishers which induced him to bring out the remaining volume.

Could not have been written by fools or for any foolish purpose. That is, I am convinced, a true presentiment to have in one's mind when one looks at Irish documents like the Book of Ballymote, or Welsh documents like the *Red Book of Hergest*. In some respects, at any rate, these documents are what they claim to be, they hold what they pretend to hold, they touch that primitive world of which they profess to be the voice. The true critic is he who can detect this precious and genuine part in them, and employ it for the elucidation of the Celt's genius and history, and for any other fruitful purposes to which it can be applied. Merely to point out the mixture of what is late and spurious in them, is to touch but the fringes of the matter. In reliance upon the discovery of this mixture of what is late and spurious in them, to pooh-pooh them altogether, to treat them as a heap of rubbish, a mass of middle-age forgeries, is to fall into the greatest possible error. Granted that all the manuscripts of Welsh poetry (to take that branch of Celtic literature which has had, in Mr. Nash, the ablest disparager), granted that all such manuscripts that we possess are, with the most insignificant exception, not older than the twelfth century; granted that the twelfth and thirteenth centuries were a time of great poetical activity in Wales, a time when the mediæval literature flourished there, as it flourished in England, France, and other countries; granted that a great deal of what Welsh enthusiasts have attributed to their great traditional poets of the sixth century belongs to this later epoch,—what then? Does that get rid of the great traditional poets,—the Cynveirdd or old bards, Aneurin, Taliesin, Llywarch Hen, and their compeers,—does that get rid of the great poetical tradition of the sixth century altogether, does it merge the whole literary antiquity of Wales in her mediæval literary antiquity, or, at least, reduce all other than this to insignificance? Mr. Nash says it does; all his efforts are directed to show how much of the so called sixth-century pieces may be resolved into mediæval, twelfth-century work; his grand thesis is that there is nothing primitive and pre-Christian in the extant Welsh literature, no traces of the Druidism and Paganism every one associates with Celtic antiquity; all this, he says, was extinguished by Paulinus in AD. 59, and never resuscitated. 'At the time the Mabinogion and the Taliesin ballads were composed, no tradition or popular recollection of the Druids or the Druidical mythology existed in Wales. The Welsh bards knew of no older mystery, nor of any mystic creed, unknown to the rest of the Christian world.' And Mr. Nash complains that 'the old opinion that the Welsh poems contain notices of Druid or Pagan superstitions of a remote origin' should still find promulgators; what we find in them is only, he says, what was circulating in Wales in the twelfth century, and one great mistake in these investigations has been the supposing that the Welsh of the twelfth, or even of the sixth century, were wiser as well as more Pagan than their neighbours.'

Why, what a wonderful thing is this! We have, in the first place, the most weighty and explicit testimony,—Strabo's, Cæsar's, Lucan's,—that this race once possessed a special, profound, spiritual discipline, that they were, to use Mr. Nash's words, 'wiser than their neighbours.' Lucan's words are singularly clear and strong, and serve well to stand as a landmark in this controversy, in which one is sometimes embarrassed by hearing authorities quoted on this side or that, when one does not feel sure precisely what they say, how much or how little; Lucan, addressing those hitherto under the pressure of Rome, but now left by the Roman civil war to their own devices, says:—

'Ye too, ye bards, who by your praises perpetuate the memory of the fallen brave, without hindrance poured forth your strains. And ye, ye Druids, now that the sword was removed, began once more your barbaric rites and weird solemnities. To you only is given knowledge or ignorance (whichever it be) of the gods and the powers of heaven; your dwelling is in the lone heart of the forest. From you we learn, that the bourne of man's ghost is not the senseless grave, not the pale realm of the monarch below; in another world his spirit survives still;—death, if your lore be true, is but the passage to enduring life.'

There is the testimony of an educated Roman, fifty years after Christ, to the Celtic race being then 'wiser than their neighbours;' testimony all the more remarkable because civilised nations, though very prone to ascribe to barbarous people an ideal purity and simplicity of life and manners, are by no means naturally inclined to ascribe to them high attainment in intellectual and spiritual things. And now, along with this testimony of Lucan's, one has to carry in mind Cæsar's remark, that the Druids, partly from a religious scruple, partly from a desire to discipline the memory of their pupils, committed nothing to writing. Well, then come the crushing defeat of the Celtic race in Britain and the Roman conquest; but the Celtic race subsisted here still, and any one can see that, while the race subsisted, the traditions of a discipline such as that of which Lucan has drawn the picture were not likely to be so very speedily 'extinguished.' The withdrawal of the Romans, the recovered independence of the native race here, the Saxon invasion, the struggle with the Saxons, were just the ground for one of those bursts of energetic national life and self-consciousness which find a voice in a burst of poets and poetry. Accordingly, to this time, to the sixth century, the universal Welsh tradition attaches the great group of British poets, Taliesin and his fellows. In the twelfth century there began for Wales, along with another burst of national life, another burst of poetry; and this burst *literary* in the stricter sense of the word,—a burst which left, for the first time, written records. It wrote the records of its predecessors, as well as of itself, and therefore Mr. Nash wants to make it the real author of the whole poetry, one may say, of the sixth century, as well as its own. No doubt one cannot produce the texts of the poetry of the sixth century; no doubt we have this only as the twelfth and succeeding centuries wrote it down; no doubt they mixed and changed it a great deal in writing it down. But, since a continuous stream of testimony shows the enduring existence and influence among the kindred Celts of Wales and Brittany, from the sixth century to the twelfth, of an old national literature, it seems certain that much of this must be traceable in the documents of the twelfth century, and the interesting thing is to trace it. It cannot be denied that there is such a continuous stream of testimony; there is Gildas in the sixth century, Nennius in the eighth, the laws of Howel in the tenth; in the eleventh, twenty or thirty years before the new literary epoch began, we hear of Rhys ap Tudor having 'brought with him from Brittany the system of the Round Table, which at home had become quite forgotten, and he restored it as it is, with regard to minstrels and bards, as it had been at Caerleon-upon-Usk, under the Emperor Arthur, in the time of the sovereignty of the race of the Cymry over the island of Britain and its adjacent islands.' Mr. Nash's own comment on this is: 'We here see the introduction of the Arthurian romance from Brittany, preceding by nearly one generation the revival of music and poetry in North Wales;' and yet he does not seem to perceive what a testimony is here to the reality, fulness, and subsistence of that primitive literature about which he is so sceptical. Then in the twelfth century testimony to this primitive literature absolutely abounds; one can quote none better than that of Giraldus de Barri, or Giraldus Cambrensis, as he is usually called. Giraldus is an excellent authority, who knew well what he was writing about, and he speaks of the Welsh bards and rhapsodists of his time as having in their possession 'ancient and authentic books' in the Welsh language. The apparatus of technical terms of poetry, again, and the elaborate poetical organisation which we find, both in Wales and Ireland, existing from the very commencement of the mediæval literary period in each, and to which no other mediæval literature, so far as I know, shows at its first beginnings anything similar, indicates surely, in these Celtic peoples, the clear and persistent tradition of an older poetical period of great development, and almost irresistibly connects itself in one's mind with the elaborate Druidic discipline which Cæsar mentions.

But perhaps the best way to get a full sense of the storied antiquity, forming as it were the background to those mediæval documents which in Mr. Nash's eyes pretty much begin and end with themselves, is to take, almost at random, a passage from such a tale as *Kilhwch and Olwen,* in the *Mabinogion,*—that charming collection, for which we owe such a debt of gratitude to Lady Charlotte Guest (to call her still by the name she bore when she made her happy entry into the world of letters), and which she so unkindly suffers to remain out of print. Almost every page of this tale points to traditions and personages of the most remote antiquity, and is instinct with the very breath of the primitive world. Search is made for Mabon, the son of Modron, who was taken when three nights old from between his mother and the wall. The seekers go first to the Ousel of Cilgwri; the Ousel had lived long enough to peck a smith's anvil down to the size of a nut, but he had never heard of Mabon. 'But there is a race of animals who were formed before me, and I will be your guide to them.' So the Ousel guides them to the Stag of Redynvre. The Stag has seen an oak sapling, in the wood where he lived, grow up to be an oak with a hundred branches, and then slowly decay down to a withered stump, yet he had never heard of Mabon. 'But I will be your guide to the place where there is an animal which was formed before I was;' and he guides them to the Owl of Cwm Cawlwyd. 'When first I came hither,' says the Owl, 'the wide valley you see was a wooded glen. And a race of men came and rooted it up. And there grew a second wood; and this wood is the third. My wings, are they not withered stumps?' Yet the Owl, in spite of his great age, had never heard of Mabon; but he offered to be guide 'to where is the oldest animal in the world, and the one that has travelled most, the Eagle of Gwern Abwy.' The Eagle was so old, that a rock, from the top of which he pecked at the stars every evening, was now not so much as a span high. He knew nothing of Mabon; but there was a monster Salmon, into whom he once struck his claws in Llyn Llyw, who might, perhaps, tell them something of him. And at last the Salmon of Llyn Llyw told them of Mabon. 'With every tide I go along the river upwards, until I come near to the walls of Gloucester, and there have I found such wrong as I never found elsewhere.' And the Salmon took Arthur's messengers on his shoulders up to the wall of the prison in Gloucester, and they delivered Mabon.

Nothing could better give that sense of primitive and pre-mediæval antiquity which to the observer with any tact for these things is, I think, clearly perceptible in these remains, at whatever time they may have been written; or better serve to check too absolute an acceptance of Mr. Nash's doctrine,—in some respects very salutary,—'that the common assumption of such remains of the date of the sixth century, has been made upon very unsatisfactory grounds.' It is true, it has; it is true, too, that, as he goes on to say, 'writers who claim for productions actually existing only in manuscripts of the twelfth, an origin in the sixth century, are called upon to demonstrate the links of evidence, either internal or external, which bridge over this great intervening period of at least five hundred years.' Then Mr. Nash continues: 'This external evidence is altogether wanting.' Not altogether, as we have seen; that assertion is a little too strong. But I am content to let it pass, because it is true, that without internal evidence in this matter the external evidence would be of no moment. But when Mr. Nash continues further: 'And the internal evidence even of the so-called historic poems themselves, is, in some instances at least, opposed to their claims to an origin in the sixth century,' and leaves the matter there, and finishes his chapter, I say that is an unsatisfactory turn to give to the matter, and a lame and impotent conclusion to his chapter; because the one interesting, fruitful question here is, not in what instances the internal evidence opposes the claims of these poems to a sixth-century origin, but in what instances it supports them, and what these sixth-century remains, thus established, signify.

So again with the question as to the mythological import of these poems. Mr. Nash seems to me to have dealt with this, too, rather in the spirit of a sturdy enemy of the Celts and their pretensions,—often enough chimerical,—than in the spirit of a disinterested man of science. 'We find in the oldest compositions in the Welsh language no traces,' he says, 'of the Druids, or of a pagan mythology.' He will not hear of there being, for instance, in these compositions, traces of the doctrine of the transmigration of souls, attributed to the Druids in such clear words by Cæsar. He is very severe upon a German scholar, long and favourably known in this country, who has already furnished several contributions to our knowledge of the Celtic race, and of whose labours the main fruit has, I believe, not yet been given us,—Mr. Meyer. He is very severe upon Mr. Meyer, for finding in one of the poems ascribed to Taliesin, 'a sacrificial hymn addressed to the god Pryd, in his character of god of the Sun.' It is not for me to pronounce for or against this notion of Mr. Meyer's. I have not the knowledge which is needed in order to make one's suffrage in these matters of any value; speaking merely as one of the unlearned public, I will confess that allegory seems to me to play, in Mr. Meyer's theories, a somewhat excessive part; Arthur and his Twelve (?) Knights of the Round Table signifying solely the year with its twelve months; Percival and the Miller signifying solely steel and the grindstone; Stonehenge and the *Gododin* put to purely calendarial purposes; the *Nibelungen*, the *Mahabharata*, and the *Iliad*, finally following the fate of the *Gododin*; all this appears to me, I will confess, a little prematurely grasped, a little unsubstantial. But that any one who knows the set of modern mythological science towards astronomical and solar myths, a set which has already justified itself in many respects so victoriously, and which is so irresistible that one can hardly now look up at the sun without having the sensations of a moth;—that any one who knows this, should find in the Welsh remains no traces of mythology, is quite astounding. Why, the heroes and heroines of the old Cymric world are all in the sky as well as in Welsh story; Arthur is the Great Bear, his harp is the constellation Lyra; Cassiopeia's chair is Llys Don, Don's Court; the daughter of Don was Arianrod, and the Northern Crown is Caer Arianrod; Gwydion was Don's son, and the Milky Way is Caer Gwydion. With Gwydion is Math, the son of Mathonwy, the 'man of illusion and phantasy;' and the moment one goes below the surface,—almost before one goes below the surface,—all is illusion and phantasy, double-meaning, and far-reaching mythological import, in the world which all these personages inhabit. What are the three hundred ravens of Owen, and the nine sorceresses of Peredur, and the dogs of Annwn the Welsh Hades, and the birds of Rhiannon, whose song was so sweet that warriors remained spell-bound for eighty years together listening to them? What is the Avanc, the water-monster, of whom every lake-side in Wales, and her proverbial speech, and her music, to this day preserve the tradition? What is Gwyn the son of Nudd, king of fairie, the ruler of the Tylwyth Teg, or family of beauty, who till the day of doom fights on every first day of May,—the great feast of the sun among the Celtic peoples,—with Gwythyr, for the fair Cordelia, the daughter of Lear? What is the wonderful mare of Teirnyon, which on the night of every first of May foaled, and no one ever knew what became of the colt? Who is the mystic Arawn, the king of Annwn, who changed semblance for a year with Pwyll, prince of Dyved, and reigned in his place? These are no mediæval personages; they belong to an older, pagan, mythological world. The very first thing that strikes one, in reading the *Mabinogion*, is how evidently the mediæval story-teller is pillaging an antiquity of which he does not fully possess the secret; he is like a peasant building his hut on the site of Halicarnassus or Ephesus; he builds, but what he builds is full of materials of which he knows not the history, or knows by a glimmering tradition merely;—stones 'not of this building,' but of an older architecture, greater, cunninger, more majestical. In the mediæval stories of no Latin or Teutonic people does this strike one as in those of the Welsh. Kilhwch, in the story, already quoted, of *Kilhwch and Olwen*, asks help at the hand of Arthur's warriors; a list of these warriors is given, which fills I know not how many pages of Lady Charlotte Guest's book; this list is a perfect treasure-house of mysterious ruins:—

'Teithi Hen, the son of Gwynham—(his domains were swallowed up by the sea, and he himself hardly escaped, and he came to Arthur, and his knife had this peculiarity, that from the time that he came there no haft would ever remain upon it, and owing to this a sickness came over him, and he pined away during the remainder of his life, and of this he died).

'Drem, the son of Dremidyd—(when the gnat arose in the morning with the sun, Drem could see it from Gelli Wic in Cornwall, as far off as Pen Blathaon in North Britain).

'Kynyr Keinvarvawc—(when he was told he had a son born, he said to his wife: Damsel, if thy son be mine, his heart will be always cold, and there will be no warmth in his hands).'

How evident, again, is the slightness of the narrator's hold upon the Twrch-Trwyth and his strange story! How manifest the mixture of known and unknown, shadowy and clear, of different layers and orders of tradition jumbled together, in the story of Bran the Blessed, a story whose personages touch a comparatively late and historic time. Bran invades Ireland, to avenge one of 'the three unhappy blows of this island,' the daily striking of Branwen by her husband Matholwch, King of Ireland. Bran is mortally wounded by a poisoned dart, and only seven men of Britain, 'the Island of the Mighty,' escape, among them Taliesin:—

'And Bran commanded them that they should cut off his head. And take you my head, said he, and bear it even unto the White Mount in London, and bury it there with the face towards France. And a long time will you be upon the road. In Harlech you will be feasting seven years, the birds of Rhiannon singing unto you the while. And all that time the head will be to you as pleasant company as it ever was when on my body. And at Gwales in Penvro you will be fourscore years, and you may remain there, and the head with you uncorrupted, until you open the door that looks towards Aber Henvelen and towards Cornwall. And after you have opened that door, there you may no longer tarry; set forth then to London to bury the head, and go straight forward.

'So they cut off his head, and those seven went forward therewith. And Branwen was the eighth with them, and they came to land at Aber Alaw in Anglesey, and they sate down to rest. And Branwen looked towards Ireland and towards the Island of the Mighty, to see if she could descry them. "Alas," said she, "woe is me that I was ever born; two islands have been destroyed because of me." Then she uttered a loud groan, and there broke her heart. And they made her a four-sided grave, and buried her upon the banks of the Alaw.

'Then they went to Harlech, and sate down to feast and to drink there; and there came three birds and began singing, and all the songs they had ever heard were harsh compared thereto; and at this feast they continued seven years. Then they went to Gwales in Penvro, and there they found a fair and regal spot overlooking the ocean, and a spacious hall was therein. And they went into the hall, and two of its doors were open, but the third door was closed, that which looked towards Cornwall. "See yonder," said Manawyddan, "is the door that we may not open." And that night they regaled themselves and were joyful. And there they remained fourscore years, nor did they think they had ever spent a time more joyous and mirthful. And they were not more weary than when first they came, neither did they, any of them, know the time they had been there. And it was as pleasant to them having the head with them as if Bran had been with them himself.

'But one day said Heilyn, the son of Gwyn: "Evil betide me if I do not open the door to know if that is true which is said concerning it." So he opened the door and looked towards Cornwall and Aber Henvelen. And when they had looked, they were as conscious of all the evils they had ever sustained, and of all the friends and companions they had lost, and of all the misery that had befallen them, as if all had happened in that very spot; and especially of the fate of their lord. And because of their perturbation they could not rest, but journeyed forth with the head towards London. And they buried the head in the White Mount.'

Arthur afterwards, in his pride and self-confidence, disinterred the head, and this was one of 'the three unhappy disclosures of the island of Britain.'

There is evidently mixed here, with the newer legend, a *detritus*, as the geologists would say, of something far older; and the secret of Wales and its genius is not truly reached until this *detritus*, instead of being called recent because it is found in contact with what is recent, is disengaged, and is made to tell its own story.

But when we show him things of this kind in the Welsh remains, Mr. Nash has an answer for us. 'Oh,' he says, 'all this is merely a machinery of necromancers and magic, such as has probably been possessed by all people in all ages, more or less abundantly. How similar are the creations of the human mind in times and places the most remote! We see in this similarity only an evidence of the existence of a common stock of ideas, variously developed according to the formative pressure of external circumstances. The materials of these tales are not peculiar to the Welsh.' And then Mr. Nash points out, with much learning and ingenuity, how certain incidents of these tales have their counterparts in Irish, in Scandinavian, in Oriental romance. He says, fairly enough, that the assertions of Taliesin, in the famous *Hanes Taliesin*, or *History of Taliesin*, that he was present with Noah in the Ark, at the Tower of Babel, and with Alexander of Macedon, 'we may ascribe to the poetic fancy of the Christian priest of the thirteenth century, who brought this romance into its present form. We may compare these statements of the universal presence of the wonder-working magician with those of the gleeman who recites the Anglo-Saxon metrical tale called the *Traveller's Song*.' No doubt, lands the most distant can be shown to have a common property in many marvellous stories. This is one of the most interesting discoveries of modern science; but modern science is equally interested in knowing how the genius of each people has differentiated, so to speak, this common property of theirs; in tracking out, in each case, that special 'variety of development,' which, to use Mr. Nash's own words, 'the formative pressure of external circumstances' has occasioned; and not the formative pressure from without only, but also the formative pressure from within. It is this which he who deals with the Welsh remains in a philosophic spirit wants to know. Where is the force, for scientific purposes, of telling us that certain incidents by which Welsh poetry has been supposed to indicate a surviving tradition of the doctrine of transmigration, are found in Irish poetry also, when Irish poetry has, like Welsh, its roots in that Celtism which is said to have held this doctrine of transmigration so strongly? Where is even the great force, for scientific purposes, of proving, if it were possible to prove, that the extant remains of Welsh poetry contain not one plain declaration of Druidical, Pagan, pre-Christian doctrine, if one has in the extant remains of Breton poetry such texts as this from the prophecy of Gwenchlan: 'Three times must we all die, before we come to our final repose'? or as the cry of the eagles, in the same poem, of fierce thirst for Christian blood, a cry in which the poet evidently gives vent to his own hatred? since the solidarity, to use that convenient French word, of Breton and Welsh poetry is so complete, that the ideas of the one may be almost certainly assumed not to have been wanting to those of the other. The question is, when Taliesin says, in the *Battle of the Trees*: 'I have been in many shapes before I attained a congenial form. I have been a narrow blade of a sword, I have been a drop in the air, I have been a shining star, I have been a word in a book, I have been a book in the beginning, I have been a light in a lantern a year and a half, I have been a bridge for passing over three-score rivers; I have journeyed as an eagle, I have been a boat on the sea, I have been a director in battle, I have been a sword in the hand, I have been a shield in fight, I have been the string of a harp, I have been enchanted for a year in the foam of water. There is nothing in which I have not been,'—the question is, have these 'statements of the universal presence of the wonder-working magician' nothing which distinguishes them from 'similar creations of the human mind in times and places the most remote;' have they not an inwardness, a severity of form, a solemnity of tone, which indicates the still reverberating echo of a profound doctrine and discipline, such as was Druidism? Suppose we compare Taliesin, as Mr. Nash invites us, with the gleeman of the Anglo-Saxon *Traveller's Song*. Take the specimen of this song which Mr. Nash himself quotes: 'I have been with the Israelites and with the Essyringi, with the Hebrews and with the Indians and with the Egyptians; I have been with the Medes and with the Persians and with the Myrgings.' It is very well to parallel with this extract Taliesin's: 'I carried the banner before Alexander; I was in Canaan when Absalom was slain; I was on the horse's crupper of Elias and Enoch; I was on the high cross of the merciful son of God; I was the chief overseer at the building of the tower of Nimrod; I was with my King in the manger of the ass; I supported Moses through the waters of Jordan; I have been in the buttery in the land of the Trinity; it is not known what is the nature of its meat and its fish.' It is very well to say that these assertions 'we may fairly ascribe to the poetic fancy of a Christian priest of the thirteenth century.' Certainly we may; the last of Taliesin's assertions more especially; though one must remark at the same time that the Welshman shows much more fire and imagination than the Anglo-Saxon. But Taliesin adds, after his: 'I was in Canaan when Absalom was slain,' '*I was in the hall of Don before Gwydion was born;*' he adds, after: 'I was chief overseer at the building of the tower of Nimrod,' '*I have been three times resident in the castle of Arianrod;*' he adds, after: 'I was at the cross with Mary Magdalene,' '*I obtained my inspiration from the cauldron of Ceridwen.*' And finally, after the mediæval touch of the visit to the buttery in the land of the Trinity, he goes off at score: 'I have been instructed in the whole system of the universe; I shall be till the day of judgment on the face of the earth. I have been in an uneasy chair above Caer Sidin, and the whirling round without motion between three elements. Is it not the wonder of the world that cannot be discovered?' And so he ends the poem. But here is the Celtic, the essential part of the poem: it is here that the 'formative pressure' has been really in operation; and here surely is paganism and mythology enough, which the Christian priest of the thirteenth century can have had nothing to do with. It is unscientific, no doubt, to interpret this part as Edward Davies and Mr. Herbert do; but it is unscientific also to get rid of it as Mr. Nash does. Wales and the Welsh genius are not to be known without this part; and the true critic is he who can best disengage its real significance.

I say, then, what we want is to *know* the Celt and his genius; not to exalt him or to abase him, but to know him. And for this a disinterested, positive, and constructive criticism is needed. Neither his friends nor his enemies have yet given us much of this. His friends have given us materials for criticism, and for these we ought to be grateful; his enemies have given us negative criticism, and for this, too, up to a certain point, we may be grateful; but the criticism we really want neither of them has yet given us.

Philology, however, that science which in our time has had so many successes, has not been abandoned by her good fortune in touching the Celt; philology has brought, almost for the first time in their lives, the Celt and sound criticism together. The Celtic grammar of Zeuss, whose death is so grievous a loss to science, offers a splendid specimen of that patient, disinterested way of treating objects of knowledge, which is the best and most attractive characteristic of Germany. Zeuss proceeds neither as a Celt-lover nor as a Celt-hater; not the slightest trace of a wish to glorify Teutonism or to abase Celtism, appears in his book. The only desire apparent there, is the desire to know his object, the language of the Celtic peoples, as it really is. In this he stands as a model to Celtic students; and it has been given to him, as a reward for his sound method, to establish certain points which are henceforth cardinal points, landmarks, in all the discussion of Celtic matters, and which no one had so established before. People talked at random of Celtic writings of this or that age; Zeuss has definitely fixed the age of what we actually have of these writings. To take the Cymric group of languages: our earliest Cornish document is a vocabulary of the thirteenth century; our earliest Breton document is a short description of an estate in a deed of the ninth century; our earliest Welsh documents are Welsh glosses of the eighth century to Eutychus, the grammarian, and Ovid's *Art of Love*, and the verses found by Edward Lhuyd in the *Juvencus* manuscript at Cambridge. The mention of this *Juvencus* fragment, by-the-by, suggests the difference there is between an interested and a disinterested critical habit. Mr. Nash deals with this fragment; but, in spite of all his great acuteness and learning, because he has a bias, because he does not bring to these matters the disinterested spirit they need, he is capable of getting rid, quite unwarrantably, of a particular word in the fragment which does not suit him; his dealing with the verses is an advocate's dealing, not a critic's. Of this sort of thing Zeuss is incapable.

The test which Zeuss used for establishing the age of these documents is a scientific test, the test of orthography and of declensional and syntactical forms. These matters are far out of my province, but what is clear, sound, and simple, has a natural attraction for us all, and one feels a pleasure in repeating it. It is the grand sign of age, Zeuss says, in Welsh and Irish words, when what the grammarians call the '*destitutio tenuium*' has not yet taken place; when the sharp consonants have not yet been changed into flat, *p* or *t* into *b* or *d*; when, for instance, *map*, a son, has not yet become *mab*; *coet* a wood, *coed*; *ocet*, a harrow, *oged*. This is a clear, scientific test to apply, and a test of which the accuracy can be verified; I do not say that Zeuss was the first person who knew this test or applied it, but I say that he is the first person who in dealing with Celtic matters has invariably proceeded by means of this and similar scientific tests; the first person, therefore, the body of whose work has a scientific, stable character; and so he stands as a model to all Celtic inquirers.

His influence has already been most happy; and as I have enlarged on a certain failure in criticism of Eugene O'Curry's,—whose business, after all, was the description and classification of materials rather than criticism,—let me show, by another example from Eugene O'Curry, this good influence of Zeuss upon Celtic studies. Eugene O'Curry wants to establish that compositions of an older date than the twelfth century existed in Ireland in the twelfth century, and thus he proceeds. He takes one of the great extant Irish manuscripts, the *Leabhar na h'Uidhre*; or, *Book of the Dun Cow*. The compiler of this book was, he says, a certain Maelmuiri, a member of the religious house of Cluainmacnois. This he establishes from a passage in the manuscript itself: 'This is a trial of his pen here, by Maelmuiri, son of the son of Conn na m'Bocht.' The date of Maelmuiri he establishes from a passage in the *Annals of the Four Masters*, under the year 1106: 'Maelmuiri, son of the son of Conn na m'Bocht, was killed in the middle of the great stone church of Cluainmacnois, by a party of robbers.' Thus he gets the date of the *Book of the Dun Cow*. This book contains an elegy on the death of St. Columb. Now, even before 1106, the language of this elegy was so old as to require a gloss to make it intelligible, for it is accompanied by a gloss written between the lines. This gloss quotes, for the explanation of obsolete words, a number of more ancient compositions; and these compositions, therefore, must, at the beginning of the twelfth century, have been still in existence. Nothing can be sounder; every step is proved, and fairly proved, as one goes along. O'Curry thus affords a good specimen of the sane mode of proceeding so much wanted in Celtic researches, and so little practised by Edward Davies and his brethren; and to found this sane method, Zeuss, by the example he sets in his own department of philology, has mainly contributed.

Science's reconciling power, too, on which I have already touched, philology, in her Celtic researches, again and again illustrates. Races and languages have been absurdly joined, and unity has been often rashly assumed at stages where one was far, very far, from having yet really reached unity. Science has and will long have to be a divider and a separatist, breaking arbitrary and fanciful connections, and dissipating dreams of a premature and impossible unity. Still, science,—true science,—recognises in the bottom of her soul a law of ultimate fusion, of conciliation. To reach this, but to reach it legitimately, she tends. She draws, for instance, towards the same idea which fills her elder and diviner sister, poetry,—the idea of the substantial unity of man; though she draws towards it by roads of her own. But continually she is showing us affinity where we imagined there was isolation. What school-boy of us has not rummaged his Greek dictionary in vain for a satisfactory account of that old name for the Peloponnese, the *Apian Land*? and within the limits of Greek itself there is none. But the Scythian name for earth 'apia,' *watery, water-issued,* meaning first *isle* and then *land*—this name, which we find in 'avia,' Scandin*avia,* and in 'ey' for Alder*ney,* not only explains the *Apian Land* of Sophocles for us, but points the way to a whole world of relationships of which we knew nothing. The Scythians themselves again,—obscure, far-separated Mongolian people as they used to appear to us,—when we find that they are essentially Teutonic and Indo-European, their very name the same word as the common Latin word 'scutum,' the *shielded* people, what a surprise they give us! And then, before we have recovered from this surprise we learn that the name of their father and god, Targitavus, carries us I know not how much further into familiar company. This divinity, *Shining with the targe,* the Greek Hercules, the Sun, contains in the second half of his name, *tavus,* 'shining,' a wonderful cement to hold times and nations together. *Tavus,* 'shining,' from 'tava'—in Sanscrit, as well as Scythian, 'to burn' or 'shine,'—is *Divus, dies, Zeus, Θεός, Dêva,* and I know not how much more; and *Taviti,* the bright and burnt, fire, the place of fire, the hearth, the centre of the family, becomes the family itself, just as our word family, the Latin *familia,* is from *thymelé,* the sacred centre of fire. The hearth comes to mean home. Then from home it comes to mean the group of homes, the tribe; from the tribe the entire nation; and in this sense of nation or people, the word appears in Gothic, Norse, Celtic, and Persian, as well as in Scythian; the *Theuthisks,* Deutschen, Tudesques, are the men of one *theuth,* nation, or people; and of this our name *Germans* itself is, perhaps, only the Roman translation, meaning the men of one germ or stock. The Celtic divinity, Teutates, has his name from the Celtic *teuta*, people; *taviti*, fire, appearing here in its secondary and derived sense of *people*, just as it does in its own Scythian language in Targitavus's second name, *Tavit-varus*, *Teutaros*, the protector of the people. Another Celtic divinity, the Hesus of Lucan, finds his brother in the Gaisos, the sword, symbolising the god of battles of the Teutonic Scythians.[8] And after philology has thus related to each other the Celt and the Teuton, she takes another branch of the Indo-European family, the Sclaves, and shows us them as having the same name with the German Suevi, the *solar* people; the common ground here, too, being that grand point of union, the sun, fire. So, also, we find Mr. Meyer, whose Celtic studies I just now mentioned, harping again and again on the connection even in Europe, if you go back far enough, between Celt and German. So, after all we have heard, and truly heard, of the diversity between all

[8] See *Les Scythes, les Ancêtres des Peuples Germaniques et Slaves,* par F. G. Bergmann, professeur à la faculté des Lettres de Strasbourg: Colmar, 1858. But Professor Bergmann's etymologies are often, says Lord Strangford, 'false lights, held by an uncertain hand.' And Lord Strangford continues:—'The Apian land certainly meant the watery land, *Meer-Umschlungon,* among the pre-Hellenic Greeks, just as the same land is called Morea by the modern post-Hellenic or Romaic Greeks from *more,* the name for the sea in the Slavonic vernacular of its inhabitants during the heart of the middle ages. But it is only connected by a remote and secondary affinity, if connected at all, with the *avia* of Scandinavia, assuming that to be the true German word for *water,* which, if it had come down to us in Gothic, would have been *avi,* genitive *aujôs,* and not a mere Latinised termination. Scythian is surely a negative rather than a positive term, much like our *Indian,* or the *Turanian* of modern ethnologists, used to comprehend nomads and barbarians of all sorts and races north and east of the Black and Caspian seas. It is unsafe to connect their name with anything as yet; it is quite as likely that it refers to the bow and arrow as to the shield, and is connected with our word to *shoot, sceótan, skiutan,* Lithuanian *szau-ti.* Some of the Scythian peoples may have been Anarian, Allophylic, Mongolian; some were demonstrably Aryan, and not only that, but Iranian as well, as is best shown in a memoir read before the Berlin Academy this last year; the evidence having been first indicated in the rough by Schaffarik the Slavonic antiquary. Coins, glosses, proper names, and inscriptions prove it. Targitaos (not -tavus) and the rest is guess-work or wrong. Herodotus's Ταβιτι for the goddess Vesta is not connected with the root *div* whence Dêvas, Deus, &c., but the root *tap,* in Latin *tep* (of tepere, tepefacere), Slavonic *tepl, topl* (for *tep* or *top*), in modern Persian *tâb. Thymele* refers to the hearth as the place of smoke (θύω, *thus, fumus*), but *familia* denotes household from *famulus* for *fagmulus,* the root *fag* being equated with the Sansk. *bhaj, servira.* Lucan's Hesus or Esus may fairly be compared with the Welsh *Hu* Gadarn by legitimate process, but no letter-change can justify his connection with *Gaisos,* the spear, not the sword, Virgil's *gæsum,* A. S. *gár,* our verb to *gore,* retained in its outer form in *gar*-fish. For *Theuthisks lege Thiudisks,* from *thiuda, populus;* in old high German Diutisk, Diotisk, *popularis, vulgaris,* the country vernacular as distinguished from the cultivated Latin; hence the word *Dutch, Deutsch.* With our ancestors *theód* stood for nation generally and *getheóde* for any speech. Our diet in the political sense is the same word, but borrowed from our German cousins, not inherited from our fathers. The modern Celtic form is the Irish *tuath,* in ancient Celtic it must have been *teuta, touta,* of which we actually have the adjective *toutius* in the Gaulish inscription of Nismes. In Oscan we have it as *turta, tuta,* its adjective being handed down in Livy's *meddix tuticus,* the mayor or chief magistrate of the *tuta.* In the Umbrian inscriptions it is *tota.* In Lithuanian *tauta,* the country opposed to the town, and in old Prussian *tauta,* the country generally, *en Prusiskan tautan, im Land zu Preussen.*'

things Semitic and all things Indo-European, there is now an Italian philologist at work upon the relationship between Sanscrit and Hebrew.

Both in small and great things, philology, dealing with Celtic matters, has exemplified this tending of science towards unity. Who has not been puzzled by the relation of the Scots with Ireland—that *vetus et major Scotia,* as Colgan calls it? Who does not feel what pleasure Zeuss brings us when he suggests that *Gael,* the name for the Irish Celt, and *Scot,* are at bottom the same word, both having their origin in a word meaning *wind,* and both signifying *the violent stormy people*?[9] Who does not feel his mind agreeably cleared about our friends the Fenians, when he learns that the root of their name, *fen,* 'white,' appears in the hero Fingal; in Gwynned, the Welsh name for North Wales in the Roman Venedotia; in Vannes in Brittany; in Venice? The very name of Ireland, some say, comes from the famous Sanscrit word *Arya,* the land of the Aryans, or noble men; although the weight of opinion seems to be in favour of connecting it rather with another Sanscrit word, *avara,* occidental, the western land or isle of the west.[10] But, at any rate, who that has been brought up to think the Celts utter aliens from us and our culture, can come without a start of sympathy upon such words as *heol* (sol), or *buaist* (fuisti)? or upon such a sentence as this, '*Peris Duw dui funnaun*' ('God prepared two fountains')? Or when Mr. Whitley Stokes, one of the very ablest scholars formed in Zeuss's school, a born philologist,—he now occupies, alas! a post under the Government of India, instead of a chair of philology at home, and makes one think mournfully of Montesquieu's saying, that had he been an Englishman he should never have produced his great work, but have caught the contagion of practical life, and devoted himself to what is called 'rising in the world,' when Mr. Whitley Stokes, in his edition of *Cormac's Glossary,* holds up the Irish word *traith,* the sea, and makes us remark that, though the names *Triton, Amphitrite,* and those of corresponding Indian and Zend divinities, point to the meaning *sea,* yet it is only Irish which actually supplies the vocable, how delightfully that brings Ireland into the Indo-European concert! What a wholesome buffet it gives to Lord Lyndhurst's alienation doctrines!

To go a little further. Of the two great Celtic divisions of language, the Gaelic and the Cymric, the Gaelic, say the philologists, is more related to the younger, more synthetic, group of languages, Sanscrit, Greek, Zend, Latin and Teutonic; the Cymric to the older, more analytic Turanian group. Of the more synthetic Aryan group, again, Zend and Teutonic are, in their turn, looser and more analytic than Sanscrit and Greek, more in sympathy with the Turanian group and with Celtic. What possibilities of affinity and influence are here hinted at; what lines of inquiry, worth exploring, at any rate, suggest themselves to one's mind. By the forms of its language a nation expresses its very self. Our language is the loosest, the most

[9] Lord Strangford observes here:—'The original forms of Gael should be mentioned—Gaedil, Goidil: in modern Gaelic orthography Gaoidheal where the *dh* is not realised in pronunciation. There is nothing impossible in the connection of the root of this with that of Scot, *if* the *s* of the latter be merely prosthetic. But the whole thing is *in nubibus,* and given as a guess only.'

[10] 'The name of Erin,' says Lord Strangford, 'is treated at length in a masterly note by Whitley Stokes in the 1st series of Max Müller's lectures (4th ed.) p. 255, where its earliest *tangible* form is shown to have been Iverio. Pictet's connection with Arya is quite baseless.'

analytic, of all European languages. And we, then, what are we? what is England? I will not answer, A vast obscure Cymric basis with a vast visible Teutonic superstructure; but I will say that that answer sometimes suggests itself, at any rate,—sometimes knocks at our mind's door for admission; and we begin to cast about and see whether it is to be let in.

But the forms of its language are not our only key to a people; what it says in its language, its literature, is the great key, and we must get back to literature. The literature of the Celtic peoples has not yet had its Zeuss, and greatly it wants him. We need a Zeuss to apply to Celtic literature, to all its vexed questions of dates, authenticity, and significance, the criticism, the sane method, the disinterested endeavour to get at the real facts, which Zeuss has shown in dealing with Celtic language. Science is good in itself, and therefore Celtic literature,—the Celt-haters having failed to prove it a bubble,—Celtic literature is interesting, merely as an object of knowledge. But it reinforces and redoubles our interest in Celtic literature if we find that here, too, science exercises the reconciling, the uniting influence of which I have said so much; if we find here, more than anywhere else, traces of kinship, and the most essential sort of kinship, spiritual kinship, between us and the Celt, of which we had never dreamed. I settle nothing, and can settle nothing; I have not the special knowledge needed for that. I have no pretension to do more than to try and awaken interest; to seize on hints, to point out indications, which, to any one with a feeling for literature, suggest themselves; to stimulate other inquirers. I must surely be without the bias which has so often rendered Welsh and Irish students extravagant; why, my very name expresses that peculiar Semitico-Saxon mixture which makes the typical Englishman; I can have no ends to serve in finding in Celtic literature more than is there. What *is* there, is for me the only question.

III.

We have seen how philology carries us towards ideas of affinity of race which are new to us. But it is evident that this affinity, even if proved, can be no very potent affair, unless it goes beyond the stage at which we have hitherto observed it. Affinity between races still, so to speak, in their mother's womb, counts for something, indeed, but cannot count for very much. So long as Celt and Teuton are in their embryo rudimentary state, or, at least, no such great while out of their cradle, still engaged in their wanderings, changes of place and struggle for development, so long as they have not yet crystallised into solid nations, they may touch and mix in passing, and yet very little come of it. It is when the embryo has grown and solidified into a distinct nation, into the Gaul or German of history, when it has finally acquired the characters which make the Gaul of history what he is, the German of history what he is, that contact and mixture are important, and may leave a long train of effects; for Celt and Teuton by this time have their formed, marked, national, ineffaceable qualities to oppose or to communicate. The contact of the German of the Continent with the Celt was in the pre-historic times, and the definite German type, as we know it, was fixed later, and from the time when it became fixed was not influenced by the Celtic type. But here in our country, in historic times, long after the Celtic embryo had crystallised into the Celt proper, long after the Germanic embryo had crystallised into the German proper, there was an important contact between the two peoples; the Saxons invaded the Britons and settled themselves in the Britons' country. Well, then, here was a contact which one might expect would leave its traces; if the Saxons got the upper hand, as we all know they did, and made our country be England and us be English, there must yet, one would think, be some trace of the Saxon having met the Briton; there must be some Celtic vein or other running through us. Many people say there is nothing at all of the kind, absolutely nothing; the *Saturday Review* treats these matters of ethnology with great power and learning, and the *Saturday Review* says we are 'a nation into which a Norman element, like a much smaller Celtic element, was so completely absorbed that it is vain to seek after Norman or Celtic elements in any modern Englishman.' And the other day at Zurich I read a long essay on English literature by one of the professors there, in which the writer observed, as a remarkable thing, that while other countries conquered by the Germans,—France, for instance, and Italy,—had ousted all German influence from their genius and literature, there were two countries, not originally Germanic, but conquered by the Germans, England and German Switzerland, of which the genius and the literature were purely and unmixedly German; and this he laid down as a position which nobody would dream of challenging.

I say it is strange that this should be so, and we in particular have reason for inquiring whether it really is so; because though, as I have said, even as a matter of science the Celt has a claim to be known, and we have an interest in knowing him, yet this interest is wonderfully enhanced if we find him to have actually a part in us. The question is to be tried by external and by internal evidence; the language and the physical type of our race afford certain data for trying it, and other data are afforded by our literature, genius, and spiritual production generally. Data of this second kind belong to the province of the literary critic; data of the first kind to the province of the philologist and of the physiologist.

The province of the philologist and of the physiologist is not mine; but this whole question as to the mixture of Celt with Saxon in us has been so little explored, people have been so prone to settle it off-hand according to their prepossessions, that even on the philological and physiological side of it I must say a few words in passing. Surely it must strike with surprise any one who thinks of it, to find that without any immense inpouring of a whole people, that by mere expeditions of invaders having to come over the sea, and in no greater numbers than the Saxons, so far as we can make out, actually came, the old occupants of this island, the Celtic Britons, should have been completely annihilated, or even so completely absorbed that it is vain to seek after Celtic elements in the existing English race. Of deliberate wholesale extermination of the Celtic race, all of them who could not fly to Wales or Scotland, we hear nothing; and without some such extermination one would suppose that a great mass of them must have remained in the country, their lot the obscure and, so to speak, underground lot of a subject race, but yet insensibly getting mixed with their conquerors, and their blood entering into the composition of a new people, in which the stock of the conquerors counts for most, but the stock of the conquered, too, counts for something. How little the triumph of the conqueror's laws, manners, and language, proves the extinction of the old race, we may see by looking at France; Gaul was Latinised in language, manners, and laws, and yet her people remained essentially Celtic. The Germanisation of Britain went far deeper than the Latinisation of France, and not only laws, manners, and language, but the main current of the blood became Germanic; but how, without some process of radica extirpation, of which, as I say, there is no evidence, can there have failed to subsist in Britain, as in Gaul, a Celtic current too? The indications of this in our language have never yet been thoroughly searched out; the Celtic names of places prove nothing, of course, as to the point here in question; they come from the pre-historic times, the times before the nations, Germanic or Celtic, had crystallised, and they are everywhere, as the impetuous Celt was formerly everywhere,—in the Alps, the Apennines, the Cevennes, the Rhine, the Po, as well as in the Thames, the Humber, Cumberland, London. But it is said that the words of Celtic origin for things having to do with every-day peaceful life,—the life of a settled nation,—words like *basket* (to take an instance which all the world knows) form a much larger body in our language than is commonly supposed; it is said that a number of our raciest, most idiomatic, popular words—for example, *bam, kick, whop, twaddle, fudge, hitch, muggy,*—are Celtic. These assertions require to be carefully examined, and it by no means follows that because an English word is found in Celtic, therefore we get it from thence; but they have not yet had the attention which, as illustrating through language this matter of the subsistence and intermingling in our nation of a Celtic part, they merit.

Nor have the physiological data which illustrate this matter had much more attention from us in England. But in France, a physician, half English by blood though a Frenchman by home and language, Monsieur W. F. Edwards, brother to Monsieur Milne-Edwards, the well-known zoologist, published in 1839 a letter to Monsieur Amédée Thierry with this title: *Des Caractères Physiologiques des Races Humaines considérés dans leurs Rapports avec l'Histoire*. The letter attracted great attention on the Continent; it fills not much more than a hundred pages, and they are a hundred pages which well deserve reading and re-reading. Monsieur Thierry in his *Histoire des Gaulois* had divided the population of Gaul into certain groups, and the object of Monsieur Edwards was to try this division by physiology. Groups of men have, he says, their physical type which distinguishes them, as well as their language; the traces of this physical type endure as the traces of language endure, and physiology is enabled to verify history by them. Accordingly, he determines the physical type of each of the two great Celtic families, the Gaels and the Cymris, who are said to have been distributed in a certain order through Gaul, and then he tracks these types in the population of France at the present day, and so verifies the alleged original order of distribution. In doing this, he makes excursions into neighbouring countries where the Gaels and the Cymris have been, and he declares that in England he finds abundant traces of the physical type which he has established as the Cymric, still subsisting in our population, and having descended from the old British possessors of our soil before the Saxon conquest. But if we are to believe the current English opinion, says Monsieur Edwards, the stock of these old British possessors is clean gone. On this opinion he makes the following comment:—

'In the territory occupied by the Saxons, the Britons were no longer an independent nation, nor even a people with any civil existence at all. For history, therefore, they were dead, above all for history as it was then written; but they had not perished; they still lived on, and undoubtedly in such numbers as the remains of a great nation, in spite of its disasters, might still be expected to keep. That the Britons were destroyed or expelled from England, properly so called, is, as I have said, a popular opinion in that country. It is founded on the exaggeration of the writers of history; but in these very writers, when we come to look closely at what they say, we find the confession that the remains of this people were reduced to a state of strict servitude. Attached to the soil, they will have shared in that emancipation which during the course of the middle ages gradually restored to political life the mass of the population in the countries of Western Europe; recovering by slow degrees their rights without resuming their name, and rising gradually with the rise of industry, they will have got spread through all ranks of society. The gradualness of this movement, and the obscurity which enwrapped its beginnings, allowed the contempt of the conqueror and the shame of the conquered to become fixed feelings; and so it turns out, that an Englishman who now thinks himself sprung from the Saxons or the Normans, is often in reality the descendant of the Britons.'

So physiology, as well as language, incomplete though the application of their tests to this matter has hitherto been, may lead us to hesitate before accepting the round assertion that it is vain to search for Celtic elements in any modern Englishman. But it is not only by the tests of physiology and language that we can try this matter. As there are for physiology physical marks, such as the square heads of the German, the round head of the Gael, the oval head of the Cymri, which determine the type of a people, so for criticism there are spiritual marks which determine the type, and make us speak of the Greek genius, the Teutonic genius, the Celtic genius, and so on. Here is another test at our service; and this test, too, has never yet been thoroughly employed. Foreign critics have indeed occasionally hazarded the idea that in English poetry there is a Celtic element traceable; and Mr. Morley, in his very readable as well as very useful book on the English writers before Chaucer, has a sentence which struck my attention when I read it, because it expresses an opinion which I, too, have long held. Mr. Morley says:—'The main current of English literature cannot be disconnected from the lively Celtic wit in which it has one of its sources. The Celts do not form an utterly distinct part of our mixed population. But for early, frequent, and various contact with the race that in its half-barbarous days invented Ossian's dialogues with St. Patrick, and that quickened afterwards the Northmen's blood in France, Germanic England would not have produced a Shakspeare.' But there Mr. Morley leaves the matter. He indicates this Celtic element and influence, but he does not show us,—it did not come within the scope of his work to show us,—how this influence has declared itself. Unlike the physiological test, or the linguistic test, this literary, spiritual test is one which I may perhaps be allowed to try my hand at applying. I say that there is a Celtic element in the English nature, as well as a Germanic element, and that this element manifests itself in our spirit and literature. But before I try to point out how it manifests itself, it may be as well to get a clear notion of what we mean by a Celtic element, a Germanic element; what characters, that is, determine for us the Celtic genius, the Germanic genius, as we commonly conceive the two.

IV.

Let me repeat what I have often said of the characteristics which mark the English spirit, the English genius. This spirit, this genius, judged, to be sure, rather from a friend's than an enemy's point of view, yet judged on the whole fairly, is characterised, I have repeatedly said, by *energy with honesty*. Take away some of the energy which comes to us, as I believe, in part from Celtic and Roman sources; instead of energy, say rather *steadiness*; and you have the Germanic genius *steadiness with honesty*. It is evident how nearly the two characterisations approach one another; and yet they leave, as we shall see, a great deal of room for difference. Steadiness with honesty; the danger for a national spirit thus composed is the humdrum, the plain and ugly, the ignoble: in a word, *das Gemeine, die Gemeinheit,* that curse of Germany, against which Goethe was all his life fighting. The excellence of a national spirit thus composed is freedom from whim, flightiness, perverseness; patient fidelity to Nature, in a word, *science,*—leading it at last, though slowly, and not by the most brilliant road, out of the bondage of the humdrum and common, into the better life. The universal dead-level of plainness and homeliness, the lack of all beauty and distinction in form and feature, the slowness and clumsiness of the language, the eternal beer, sausages, and bad tobacco, the blank commonness everywhere, pressing at last like a weight on the spirits of the traveller in Northern Germany, and making him impatient to be gone, this is the weak side; the industry, the well-doing, the patient steady elaboration of things, the idea of science governing all departments of human activity—this is the strong side; and through this side of her genius, Germany has already obtained excellent results, and is destined, we may depend upon it, however her pedantry, her slowness, her fumbling, her ineffectiveness, her bad government, may at times make us cry out, to an immense development.[11]

For dulness, the creeping Saxons,—says an old Irish poem, assigning the characteristics for which different nations are celebrated:—

> For acuteness and valour, the Greeks,
> For excessive pride, the Romans,
> For dulness, the creeping Saxons;
> For beauty and amorousness, the Gaedhils.

We have seen in what sense, and with what explanation, this characterisation of the German may be allowed to stand; now let us come to the beautiful and amorous Gaedhil. Or rather, let us find a definition which may suit both branches of the Celtic family, the Cymri as well as the Gael. It is clear that special circumstances may have developed some one side in the national character of Cymri or Gael, Welshman or Irishman, so that the observer's notice shall be readily caught by this

[11] It is to be remembered that the above was written before the recent war between Prussia and Austria.

side, and yet it may be impossible to adopt it as characteristic of the Celtic nature generally. For instance, in his beautiful essay on the poetry of the Celtic races, M. Renan, with his eyes fixed on the Bretons and the Welsh, is struck with the timidity, the shyness, the delicacy of the Celtic nature, its preference for a retired life, its embarrassment at having to deal with the great world. He talks of the *douce petite race naturellement chrétienne,* his *race fière et timide, à l'extérieur gauche et embarrassée.* But it is evident that this description, however well it may do for the Cymri, will never do for the Gael, never do for the typical Irishman of Donnybrook fair. Again, M. Renan's *infinie délicatesse de sentiment qui caractérise la race Celtique,* how little that accords with the popular conception of an Irishman who wants to borrow money! *Sentiment* is, however, the word which marks where the Celtic races really touch and are one; sentimental, if the Celtic nature is to be characterised by a single term, is the best term to take. An organisation quick to feel impressions, and feeling them very strongly; a lively personality therefore, keenly sensitive to joy and to sorrow; this is the main point. If the downs of life too much outnumber the ups, this temperament, just because it is so quickly and nearly conscious of all impressions, may no doubt be seen shy and wounded; it may be seen in wistful regret, it may be seen in passionate, penetrating melancholy; but its essence is to aspire ardently after life, light, and emotion, to be expansive, adventurous, and gay. Our word *gay,* it is said, is itself Celtic. It is not from *gaudium,* but from the Celtic *gair,* to laugh;[12] and the impressionable Celt, soon up and soon down, is the more down because it is so his nature to be up to be sociable, hospitable, eloquent, admired, figuring away brilliantly. He loves bright colours, he easily becomes audacious, overcrowing, full of fanfaronade. The German, say the physiologists, has the larger volume of intestines (and who that has ever seen a German at a table-d'hôte will not readily believe this?), the Frenchman has the more developed organs of respiration. That is just the expansive, eager Celtic nature; the head in the air, snuffing and snorting; *a proud look and a high stomach,* as the Psalmist says, but without any such settled savage temper as the Psalmist seems to impute by those words. For good and for bad, the Celtic genius is more airy and unsubstantial, goes less near the ground, than the German. The Celt is often called sensual; but it is not so much the vulgar satisfactions of sense that attract him as emotion and excitement; he is truly, as I began by saying, sentimental.

Sentimental,—*always ready to react against the despotism of fact;* that is the description a great friend[13] of the Celt gives of him; and it is not a bad description of the sentimental temperament; it lets us into the secret of its dangers and of its habitual want of success. Balance, measure, and patience, these are the eternal conditions, even supposing the happiest temperament to start with, of high success; and balance, measure, and patience are just what the Celt has never had. Even in

[12] The etymology is Monsieur Henri Martin's, but Lord Strangford says—'Whatever *gai* may be, it is assuredly not Celtic. Is there any authority for this word *gair,* to laugh, or rather "laughter," beyond O'Reilly? O'Reilly is no authority at all except in so far as tested and passed by the new school. It is hard to give up *gavisus.* But Diez, chief authority in Romanic matters, is content to accept Muratori's reference to an old High-German *gâhi,* modern *jähe,* sharp, quick, sudden, brisk, and so to the sense of lively, animated, high in spirits.'

[13] Monsieur Henri Martin, whose chapters on the Celts, in his *Histoire de France,* are full of information and interest.

the world of spiritual creation, he has never, in spite of his admirable gifts of quick perception and warm emotion, succeeded perfectly, because he never has had steadiness, patience, sanity enough to comply with the conditions under which alone can expression be perfectly given to the finest perceptions and emotions. The Greek has the same perceptive, emotional temperament as the Celt; but he adds to this temperament the sense of *measure*; hence his admirable success in the plastic arts, in which the Celtic genius, with its chafing against the despotism of fact, its perpetual straining after mere emotion, has accomplished nothing. In the comparatively petty art of ornamentation, in rings, brooches, crosiers, relic-cases, and so on, he has done just enough to show his delicacy of taste, his happy temperament; but the grand difficulties of painting and sculpture, the prolonged dealings of spirit with matter, he has never had patience for. Take the more spiritual arts of music and poetry. All that emotion alone can do in music the Celt has done; the very soul of emotion breathes in the Scotch and Irish airs; but with all this power of musical feeling, what has the Celt, so eager for emotion that he has not patience for science, effected in music, to be compared with what the less emotional German, steadily developing his musical feeling with the science of a Sebastian Bach or a Beethoven, has effected? In poetry, again, poetry which the Celt has so passionately, so nobly loved; poetry where emotion counts for so much, but where reason, too, reason, measure, sanity, also count for so much,—the Celt has shown genius, indeed, splendid genius; but even here his faults have clung to him, and hindered him from producing great works, such as other nations with a genius for poetry,—the Greeks, say, or the Italians,—have produced. The Celt has not produced great poetical works, he has only produced poetry with an air of greatness investing it all, and sometimes giving, moreover, to short pieces, or to passages, lines, and snatches of long pieces, singular beauty and power. And yet he loved poetry so much that he grudged no pains to it; but the true art, the *architectonicé* which shapes great works, such as the *Agamemnon* or the *Divine Comedy*, comes only after a steady, deep-searching survey, a firm conception of the facts of human life, which the Celt has not patience for. So he runs off into technic, where he employs the utmost elaboration, and attains astonishing skill; but in the contents of his poetry you have only so much interpretation of the world as the first dash of a quick, strong perception, and then sentiment, infinite sentiment, can bring you. Here, too, his want of sanity and steadfastness has kept the Celt back from the highest success.

If his rebellion against fact has thus lamed the Celt even in spiritual work, how much more must it have lamed him in the world of business and politics! The skilful and resolute appliance of means to ends which is needed both to make progress in material civilisation, and also to form powerful states, is just what the Celt has least turn for. He is sensual, as I have said, or at least sensuous; loves bright colours, company, and pleasure; and here he is like the Greek and Latin races; but compare the talent the Greek and Latin (or Latinised) races have shown for gratifying their senses, for procuring an outward life, rich, luxurious, splendid, with the Celt's failure to reach any material civilisation sound and satisfying, and not out at elbows, poor, slovenly, and half-barbarous. The sensuousness of the Greek made Sybaris and Corinth, the sensuousness of the Latin made Rome and Baiæ, the sensuousness of the Latinised Frenchman makes Paris; the sensuousness of the Celt proper has made Ireland. Even in his ideal heroic times, his gay and sensuous nature cannot carry him, in the appliances of his favourite life of sociability and pleasure, beyond the gross and creeping Saxon whom he despises; the regent Breas, we are told in the *Battle of Moytura of the Fomorians*, became unpopular because 'the knives of his people were not greased at his table, nor did their breath smell of ale at the banquet.' In its grossness and barbarousness is not that Saxon, as Saxon as it can be? just what the Latinised Norman, sensuous and sociable like the Celt, but with the talent to make this bent of his serve to a practical embellishment of his mode of living, found so disgusting in the Saxon.

And as in material civilisation he has been ineffectual, so has the Celt been ineffectual in politics. This colossal, impetuous, adventurous wanderer, the Titan of the early world, who in primitive times fills so large a place on earth's scene, dwindles and dwindles as history goes on, and at last is shrunk to what we now see him. For ages and ages the world has been constantly slipping, ever more and more out of the Celt's grasp. 'They went forth to the war,' Ossian says most truly, *'but they always fell.'*

And yet, if one sets about constituting an ideal genius, what a great deal of the Celt does one find oneself drawn to put into it! Of an ideal genius one does not want the elements, any of them, to be in a state of weakness; on the contrary, one wants all of them to be in the highest state of power; but with a law of measure, of harmony, presiding over the whole. So the sensibility of the Celt, if everything else were not sacrificed to it, is a beautiful and admirable force. For sensibility, the power of quick and strong perception and emotion, is one of the very prime constituents of genius, perhaps its most positive constituent; it is to the soul what good senses are to the body, the grand natural condition of successful activity. Sensibility gives genius its materials; one cannot have too much of it, if one can but keep its master and not be its slave. Do not let us wish that the Celt had had less sensibility, but that he had been more master of it. Even as it is, if his sensibility has been a source of weakness to him, it has been a source of power too, and a source of happiness. Some people have found in the Celtic nature and its sensibility the main root out of which chivalry and romance and the glorification of a feminine ideal spring; this is a great question, with which I cannot deal here. Let me notice in passing, however, that there is, in truth, a Celtic air about the extravagance of chivalry, its reaction against the despotism of fact, its straining human nature further than it will stand. But putting all this question of chivalry and its origin on one side, no doubt the sensibility of the Celtic nature, its nervous exaltation, have something feminine in them, and the Celt is thus peculiarly disposed to feel the spell of the feminine idiosyncrasy; he has an affinity to it; he is not far from its secret. Again, his sensibility gives him a peculiarly near and intimate feeling of nature and the life of nature; here, too, he seems in a special way attracted by the secret before him, the secret of natural beauty and natural magic, and to be close to it, to half-divine it. In the productions of the Celtic genius, nothing, perhaps, is so interesting as the evidences of this power: I shall have occasion to give specimens of them by-and-by. The same sensibility made the Celts full of reverence and enthusiasm for genius, learning, and the things of the mind; *to be a bard, freed a man,*—that is a characteristic stroke of this generous and ennobling ardour of theirs, which no race has ever shown more strongly. Even the extravagance and exaggeration of the sentimental Celtic nature has often something romantic and attractive about it, something which has a sort of smack of misdirected good. The Celt, undisciplinable, anarchical, and turbulent by nature, but out of affection and admiration giving himself body and soul to some leader, that is not a promising political temperament, it is just the opposite of the Anglo-Saxon temperament, disciplinable and steadily obedient within certain limits, but retaining an inalienable part of freedom and self-dependence; but it is a temperament for which one has a kind of sympathy notwithstanding. And very often, for the gay defiant reaction against fact of the lively Celtic nature one has more than sympathy; one feels, in spite of the extravagance, in spite of good sense disapproving, magnetised and exhilarated by it. The Gauls had a rule inflicting a fine on every warrior who, when he appeared on parade, was found to stick out too much in front,—to be corpulent, in short. Such a rule is surely the maddest article of war ever framed, and to people to whom nature has assigned a large volume of intestines, must appear, no doubt, horrible; but yet has it not an audacious, sparkling, immaterial manner with it, which lifts one out of routine, and sets one's spirits in a glow?

All tendencies of human nature are in themselves vital and profitable; when they are blamed, they are only to be blamed relatively, not absolutely. This holds true of the Saxon's phlegm as well as of the Celt's sentiment. Out of the steady humdrum habit of the creeping Saxon, as the Celt calls him,—out of his way of going near the ground,—has come, no doubt, Philistinism, that plant of essentially Germanic growth, flourishing with its genuine marks only in the German fatherland, Great Britain and her colonies, and the United States of America; but what a soul of goodness there is in Philistinism itself! and this soul of goodness I, who am often supposed to be Philistinism's mortal enemy merely because I do not wish it to have things all its own way, cherish as much as anybody. This steady-going habit leads at last, as I have said, up to science, up to the comprehension and interpretation of the world. With us in Great Britain, it is true, it does not seem to lead so far as that; it is in Germany, where the habit is more unmixed, that it can lead to science. Here with us it seems at a certain point to meet with a conflicting force, which checks it and prevents its pushing on to science; but before reaching this point what conquests has it not won! and all the more, perhaps, for stopping short at this point, for spending its exertions within a bounded field, the field of plain sense, of direct practical utility. How it has augmented the comforts and conveniences of life for us! Doors that open, windows that shut, locks that turn, razors that shave, coats that wear, watches that go, and a thousand more such good things, are the invention of the Philistines.

Here, then, if commingling there is in our race, are two very unlike elements to commingle; the steady-going Saxon temperament and the sentimental Celtic temperament. But before we go on to try and verify, in our life and literature, the alleged fact of this commingling, we have yet another element to take into account, the Norman element. The critic in the *Saturday Review*, whom I have already quoted, says that in looking for traces of Normanism in our national genius, as in looking for traces of Celtism in it, we do but lose our labour; he says, indeed, that there went to the original making of our nation a very great deal more of a Norman element than of a Celtic element, but he asserts that both elements have now so completely disappeared, that it is vain to look for any trace of either of them in the modern Englishman. But this sort of assertion I do not like to admit without trying it a little. I want, therefore, to get some plain notion of the Norman habit and genius, as I have sought to get some plain notion of the Saxon and Celtic. Some people will say that the Normans are Teutonic, and that therefore the distinguishing characters of the German genius must be those of their genius also; but the matter cannot be settled in this speedy fashion. No doubt the basis of the Norman race is Teutonic; but the governing point in the history of the Norman race,—so far, at least, as we English have to do with it,—is not its Teutonic origin, but its Latin civilisation. The French people have, as I have already remarked, an undoubtedly Celtic basis, yet so decisive in its effect upon a nation's habit and character can be the contact with a stronger civilisation, that Gaul, without changing the basis of her blood, became, for all practical intents and purposes, a Latin country, France and not Ireland, through the Roman conquest. Latinism conquered Celtism in her, as it also conquered the Germanism imported by the Frankish and other invasions; Celtism is, however, I need not say, everywhere manifest still in the French nation; even Germanism is distinctly traceable in it, as any one who attentively compares the French with other Latin races will see. No one can look carefully at the French troops in Rome, amongst the Italian population, and not perceive this trace of Germanism; I do not mean in the Alsatian soldiers only, but in the soldiers of genuine France. But the governing character of France, as a power in the world, is Latin; such was the force of Greek and Roman civilisation upon a race whose whole mass remained Celtic, and where the Celtic language still lingered on, they say, among the common people, for some five or six centuries after the Roman conquest. But the Normans in Neustria lost their old Teutonic language in a wonderfully short time; when they conquered England they were already Latinised; with them were a number of Frenchmen by race, men from Anjou and Poitou, so they brought into England more non-Teutonic blood, besides what they had themselves got by intermarriage, than is commonly supposed; the great point, however, is, that by civilisation this vigorous race, when it took possession of England, was Latin.

These Normans, who in Neustria had lost their old Teutonic tongue so rapidly, kept in England their new Latin tongue for some three centuries. It was Edward the Third's reign before English came to be used in law-pleadings and spoken at court. Why this difference? Both in Neustria and in England the Normans were a handful; but in Neustria, as Teutons, they were in contact with a more advanced civilisation than their own; in England, as Latins, with a less advanced. The Latinised Normans in England had the sense for fact, which the Celts had not; and the love of strenuousness, clearness, and rapidity, the high Latin spirit, which the Saxons had not. They hated the slowness and dulness of the creeping Saxon; it offended their clear, strenuous talent for affairs, as it offended the Celt's quick and delicate perception. The Normans had the Roman talent for affairs, the Roman decisiveness in emergencies. They have been called prosaic, but this is not a right word for them; they were neither sentimental, nor, strictly speaking, poetical. They had more sense for rhetoric than for poetry, like the Romans; but, like the Romans, they had too high a spirit not to like a noble intellectual stimulus of some kind, and thus they were carried out of the region of the merely prosaic. Their foible,—the bad excess of their characterising quality of strenuousness,—was not a prosaic flatness, it was hardness and insolence.

I have been obliged to fetch a very wide circuit, but at last I have got what I went to seek. I have got a rough, but, I hope, clear notion of these three forces, the Germanic genius, the Celtic genius, the Norman genius. The Germanic genius has steadiness as its main basis, with commonness and humdrum for its defect, fidelity to nature for its excellence. The Celtic genius, sentiment as its main basis, with love of beauty, charm, and spirituality for its excellence, ineffectualness and self-will for its defect. The Norman genius, talent for affairs as its main basis, with strenuousness and clear rapidity for its excellence, hardness and insolence for its defect. And now to try and trace these in the composite English genius.

V.

To begin with what is more external. If we are so wholly Anglo-Saxon and Germanic as people say, how comes it that the habits and gait of the German language are so exceedingly unlike ours? Why while the *Times* talks in this fashion: 'At noon a long line of carriages extended from Pall Mall to the Peers' entrance of the Palace of Westminster,' does the *Cologne Gazette* talk in this other fashion: 'Nachdem die Vorbereitungen zu dem auf dem GürzenichSaale zu Ebren der Abgeordneten Statt finden sollenden Bankette bereits vollständig getroffen worden waren, fand heute vormittag auf polizeiliche Anordnung die Schliessung sämmtlicher Zugänge zum Gürzenich Statt'?[14] Surely the mental habit of people who express their thoughts in so very different a manner, the one rapid, the other slow, the one plain, the other embarrassed, the one trailing, the other striding, cannot be essentially the same. The English language, strange compound as it is, with its want of inflections, and with all the difficulties which this want of inflections brings upon it, has yet made itself capable of being, in good hands, a business-instrument as ready, direct, and clear, as French or Latin. Again: perhaps no nation, after the Greeks and Romans, has so clearly felt in what true rhetoric, rhetoric of the best kind, consists, and reached so high a pitch of excellence in this, as the English. Our sense for rhet-

[14] The above is really a sentence taken from the *Cologne Gazette*. Lord Strangford's comment here is as follows:—'Modern Germanism, in a general estimate of Germanism, should not be taken, absolutely and necessarily, as the constant, whereof we are the variant. The Low-Dutch of Holland, anyhow, are indisputably as genuine Dutch as the High-Dutch of Germany Proper. But do they write sentences like this one—*informe, ingens, cui lumen ademptum*? If not, the question must be asked, not how we have come to deviate, but how the Germans have come to deviate. Our modern English prose in plain matters is often all just the same as the prose of *King Alfred* and the *Chronicle*. Ohthere's *North Sea Voyage* and Wulfstan's *Baltic Voyage* is the sort of thing which is sent in every day, one may say, to the Geographical or Ethnological Society, in the whole style and turn of phrase and thought.'

The mass of a stock must supply our data for judging the stock. But see, moreover, what I have said at p. 40.

oric has in some ways done harm to us in our cultivation of literature, harm to us, still more, in our cultivation of science; but in the true sphere of rhetoric, in public speaking, this sense has given us orators whom I do think we may, without fear of being contradicted and accused of blind national vanity, assert to have inherited the great Greek and Roman oratorical tradition more than the orators of any other country. Strafford, Bolingbroke, the two Pitts, Fox,—to cite no other names,—I imagine few will dispute that these call up the notion of an oratory, in kind, in extent, in power, coming nearer than any other body of modern oratory to the oratory of Greece and Rome. And the affinity of spirit in our best public life and greatest public men to those of Rome, has often struck observers, foreign as well as English. Now, not only have the Germans shown no eminent aptitude for rhetoric such as the English have shown,—that was not to be expected, since our public life has done so much to develop an aptitude of this kind, and the public life of the Germans has done so little,—but they seem in a singular degree devoid of any aptitude at all for rhetoric. Take a speech from the throne in Prussia, and compare it with a speech from the throne in England. Assuredly it is not in speeches from the throne that English rhetoric or any rhetoric shows its best side;—they are often cavilled at, often justly cavilled at;—no wonder, for this form of composition is beset with very trying difficulties. But what is to be remarked is this;—a speech from the throne falls essentially within the sphere of rhetoric, it is one's sense of rhetoric which has to fix its tone and style, so as to keep a certain note always sounding in it; in an English speech from the throne, whatever its faults, this rhetorical note is always struck and kept to; in a Prussian speech from the throne, never. An English speech from the throne is rhetoric; a Prussian speech is half talk,—heavy talk,—and half effusion. This is one instance, it may be said; true, but in one instance of this kind the presence or the absence of an aptitude for rhetoric is decisively shown. Well, then, why am I not to say that we English get our rhetorical sense from the Norman element in us,—our turn for this strenuous, direct, high-spirited talent of oratory, from the influence of the strenuous, direct, high-spirited Normans? Modes of life, institutions, government, and other such causes, are sufficient, I shall be told, to account for English oratory. Modes of life, institutions, government, climate, and so forth,—let me say it once for all,—will further or hinder the development of an aptitude, but they will not by themselves create the aptitude or explain it. On the other hand, a people's habit and complexion of nature go far to determine its modes of life, institutions, and government, and even to prescribe the limits within which the influences of climate shall tell upon it.

However, it is not my intention, in these remarks, to lay it down for certain that this or that part of our powers, shortcomings, and behaviour, is due to a Celtic, German, or Norman element in us. To establish this I should need much wider limits, and a knowledge, too, far beyond what I possess; all I purpose is to point out certain correspondences, not yet, perhaps, sufficiently observed and attended to, which seem to lead towards certain conclusions. The following up the inquiry till full proof is reached,—or perhaps, full disproof,—is what I want to suggest to more competent persons. Premising this, I now go on to a second matter, somewhat more delicate and inward than that with which I began. Every one knows how well the Greek and Latin races, with their direct sense for the visible, palpable world, have succeeded in the plastic arts. The sheer German races, too, with their honest love of fact, and their steady pursuit of it,—their fidelity to nature, in short,—have attained a high degree of success in these arts; few people will deny that Albert Dürer and Rubens, for example, are to be called masters in painting, and in the high kind of painting. The Celtic races, on the other hand, have shown a singular inaptitude for the plastic arts; the abstract, severe character of the Druidical religion, its dealing with the eye of the mind rather than the eye of the body, its having no elaborate temples and beautiful idols, all point this way from the first; its sentiment cannot satisfy itself, cannot even find a resting-place for itself, in colour and form; it presses on to the impalpable, the ideal. The forest of trees and the forest of rocks, not hewn timber and carved stones, suit its aspirations for something not to be bounded or expressed. With this tendency, the Celtic races have, as I remarked before, been necessarily almost impotent in the higher branches of the plastic arts. Ireland, that has produced so many powerful spirits, has produced no great sculptors or painters. Cross into England. The inaptitude for the plastic art strikingly diminishes, as soon as the German, not the Celtic element, preponderates in the race. And yet in England, too, in the English race, there is something which seems to prevent our reaching real mastership in the plastic arts, as the more unmixed German races have reached it. Reynolds and Turner are painters of genius, who can doubt it? but take a European jury, the only competent jury in these cases, and see if you can get a verdict giving them the rank of masters, as this rank is given to Raphael and Correggio, or to Albert Dürer and Rubens. And observe in what points our English pair succeed, and in what they fall short. They fall short in *architectonicé*, in the highest power of composition, by which painting accomplishes the very uttermost which it is given to painting to accomplish; the highest sort of composition, the highest application of the art of painting, they either do not attempt, or they fail in it. Their defect, therefore, is on the side of art, of plastic art. And they succeed in magic, in beauty, in grace, in expressing almost the inexpressible: here is the charm of Reynolds's children and Turner's seas; the impulse to express the inexpressible carries Turner so far, that at last it carries him away, and even long before he is quite carried away, even in works that are justly extolled, one can see the stamp-mark, as the French say, of insanity. The excellence, therefore, the success, is on the side of spirit. Does not this look as if a Celtic stream met the main German current in us, and gave it a somewhat different course from that which it takes naturally? We have Germanism enough in us, enough patient love for fact and matter, to be led to attempt the plastic arts, and we make much more way in them than the pure Celtic races make; but at a certain point our Celtism comes in, with its love of emotion, sentiment, the inexpressible, and gives our best painters a bias. And the point at which it comes in is just that critical point where the flowering of art into its perfection commences; we have plenty of painters who never reach this point at all, but remain always mere journeymen, in bondage to matter; but those who do reach it, instead of going on to the true consummation of the masters in painting, are a little overbalanced by soul and feeling, work too directly for these, and so do not get out of their art all that may be got out of it.

The same modification of our Germanism by another force which seems Celtic, is visible in our religion. Here, too, we may trace a gradation between Celt, Englishman, and German, the difference which distinguishes Englishman from German appearing attributable to a Celtic element in us. Germany is the land of exegesis, England is the land of Puritanism. The religion of Wales is more emotional and sentimental than English Puritanism; Romanism has indeed given way to Calvinism among the Welsh,—the one superstition has supplanted the other,—but the Celtic sentiment which made the Welsh such devout Catholics, remains, and gives unction to their Methodism; theirs is not the controversial, rationalistic, intellectual side of Protestantism, but the devout, emotional, religious side. Among the Germans, Protestantism has been carried on into rationalism and science. The English hold a middle place between the Germans and the Welsh; their religion has the exterior forms and apparatus of a rationalism, so far their Germanic nature carries them; but long before they get to science, their feeling, their Celtic element catches them, and turns their religion all towards piety and unction. So English Protestantism has the outside appearance of an intellectual system, and the inside reality of an emotional system: this gives it its tenacity and force, for what is held with the ardent attachment of feeling is believed to have at the same time the scientific proof of reason. The English Puritan, therefore (and Puritanism is the characteristic form of English Protestantism), stands between the German Protestant and the Celtic Methodist; his real affinity indeed, at present, being rather with his Welsh kinsman, if kinsman he may be called, than with his German.

Sometimes one is left in doubt from whence the check and limit to Germanism in us proceeds, whether from a Celtic source or from a Norman source. Of the true steady-going German nature the bane is, as I remarked, flat commonness; there seems no end to its capacity for platitude; it has neither the quick perception of the Celt to save it from platitude, nor the strenuousness of the Norman; it is only raised gradually out of it by science, but it jogs through almost interminable platitudes first. The English nature is not raised to science, but something in us, whether Celtic or Norman, seems to set a bound to our advance in platitude, to make us either shy of platitude, or impatient of it. I open an English reading-book for children, and I find these two characteristic stories in it, one of them of English growth, the other of German. Take the English story first:—

'A little boy accompanied his elder sister while she busied herself with the labours of the farm, asking questions at every step, and learning the lessons of life without being aware of it.

'"Why, dear Jane," he said, "do you scatter good grain on the ground; would it not be better to make good bread of it than to throw it to the greedy chickens?"

'"In time," replied Jane, "the chickens will grow big, and each of them will fetch money at the market. One must think on the end to be attained without counting trouble, and learn to wait."

'Perceiving a colt, which looked eagerly at him, the little boy cried out: "Jane, why is the colt not in the fields with the labourers helping to draw the carts?"

'"The colt is young," replied Jane, "and he must lie idle till he gets the necessary strength; one must not sacrifice the future to the present."'

The reader will say that is most mean and trivial stuff, the vulgar English nature in full force; just such food as the Philistine would naturally provide for his young. He will say he can see the boy fed upon it growing up to be like his father, to be all for business, to despise culture, to go through his dull days, and to die without having ever lived. That may be so; but now take the German story (one of Krummacher's), and see the difference:—

'There lived at the court of King Herod a rich man who was the king's chamberlain. He clothed himself in purple and fine linen, and fared like the king himself.

'Once a friend of his youth, whom he had not seen for many years, came from a distant land to pay him a visit. Then the chamberlain invited all his friends and made a feast in honour of the stranger.

'The tables were covered with choice food placed on dishes of gold and silver, and the finest wines of all kinds. The rich man sat at the head of the table, glad to do the honours to his friend who was seated at his right hand. So they ate and drank, and were merry.

'Then the stranger said to the chamberlain of King Herod: "Riches and splendour like thine are nowhere to be found in my country." And he praised his greatness, and called him happy above all men on earth.

'Well, the rich man took an apple from a golden vessel. The apple was large, and red, and pleasant to the eye. Then said be: "Behold, this apple hath rested on gold, and its form is very beautiful." And he presented it to the stranger, the friend of his youth. The stranger cut the apple in two; and behold, in the middle of it there was a worm!

'Then the stranger looked at the chamberlain; and the chamberlain bent his eyes on the ground and sighed.'

There it ends. Now I say, one sees there an abyss of platitude open, and the German nature swimming calmly about in it, which seems in some way or other to have its entry screened off for the English nature. The English story leads with a direct issue into practical life: a narrow and dry practical life, certainly, but yet enough to supply a plain motive for the story; the German story leads simply nowhere except into bathos. Shall we say that the Norman talent for affairs saves us here, or the Celtic perceptive instinct? one of them it must be, surely. The Norman turn seems most germane to the matter here immediately in hand; on the other hand, the Celtic turn, or some degree of it, some degree of its quick perceptive instinct, seems necessary to account for the full difference between the German nature and ours. Even in Germans of genius or talent the want of quick light tact, of instinctive perception of the impropriety or impossibility of certain things, is singularly remarkable. Herr Gervinus's prodigious discovery about Handel being an Englishman and Shakspeare a German, the incredible mare's-nest Goethe finds in looking for the origin of Byron's Manfred,—these are things from which no deliberate care or reflection can save a man; only an instinct can save him from them, an instinct that they are absurd; who can imagine Charles Lamb making Herr Gervinus's blunder, or Shakspeare making Goethe's? but from the sheer German nature this intuitive tact seems something so alien, that even genius fails to give it. And yet just what constitutes special power and genius in a man seems often to be his blending with the basis of his national temperament, some additional gift or grace not proper to that temperament; Shakspeare's greatness is thus in his blending an openness and flexibility of spirit, not English, with the English basis; Addison's, in his blending a moderation and delicacy, not English, with the English basis; Burke's in his blending a largeness of view and richness of thought, not English, with the English basis. In Germany itself, in the same way, the greatness of their great Frederic lies in his blending a rapidity and clearness, not German, with the German basis; the greatness of Goethe in his blending a love of form, nobility, and dignity,—the grand style,—with the German basis. But the quick, sure, instinctive perception of the incongruous and absurd not even genius seems to give in Germany; at least, I can think of only one German of genius, Lessing (for Heine was a Jew, and the Jewish temperament is quite another thing from the German), who shows it in an eminent degree.

If we attend closely to the terms by which foreigners seek to hit off the impression which we and the Germans make upon them, we shall detect in these terms a difference which makes, I think, in favour of the notion I am propounding. Nations in hitting off one another's characters are apt, we all know, to seize the unflattering side rather than the flattering; the mass of mankind always do this, and indeed they really see what is novel, and not their own, in a disfiguring light. Thus we ourselves, for instance, popularly say 'the phlegmatic Dutchman' rather than 'the sensible Dutchman,' or 'the grimacing Frenchman' rather than 'the polite Frenchman.' Therefore neither we nor the Germans should exactly accept the description strangers give of us, but it is enough for my purpose that strangers, in characterising us with a certain shade of difference, do at any rate make it clear that there appears this shade of difference, though the character itself, which they give us both, may be a caricature rather than a faithful picture of us. Now it is to be noticed that those sharp observers, the French,—who have a double turn for sharp observation, for they have both the quick perception of the Celt and the Latin's gift for coming plump upon the fact,—it is to be noticed, I say, that the French put a curious distinction in their popular, depreciating, we will hope inadequate, way of hitting off us and the Germans. While they talk of the '*bêtise* allemande,' they talk of the '*gaucherie* anglaise;' while they talk of the 'Allemand *balourd*,' they talk of the 'Anglais *empêtré*;' while they call the German '*niais*,' they call the Englishman '*mélancolique*.' The difference between the epithets *balourd* and *empêtré* exactly gives the difference in character I wish to seize; *balourd* means heavy and dull, *empêtré* means hampered and embarrassed. This points to a certain mixture and strife of elements in the Englishman; to the clashing of a Celtic quickness of perception with a Germanic instinct for going steadily along close to the ground. The Celt, as we have seen, has not at all, in spite of his quick perception, the Latin talent for dealing with the fact, dexterously managing it and making himself master of it; Latin or Latinised people have felt contempt for him on this account, have treated him as a poor creature, just as the German, who arrives at fact in a different way from the Latins, but who arrives at it, has treated him. The couplet of Chrestien of Troyes about the Welsh:—

> . . . Gallois sont tous, par nature,
> Plus fous que bêtes en pâsture—

is well known, and expresses the genuine verdict of the Latin mind on the Celts. But the perceptive instinct of the Celt feels and anticipates, though he has that in him which cuts him off from command of the world of fact; he sees what is wanting to him well enough; his mere eye is not less sharp, nay, it is sharper, than the Latin's. He is a quick genius, checkmated for want of strenuousness or else patience. The German has not the Latin's sharp precise glance on the world of fact, and dexterous behaviour in it; he fumbles with it much and long, but his honesty and patience give him the rule of it in the long run,—a surer rule, some of us think, than the Latin gets; still, his behaviour in it is not quick and dexterous. The Englishman, in so far as he is German,—and he is mainly German,—proceeds in the steady-going German fashion; if he were all German he would proceed thus for ever without self-consciousness or embarrassment; but, in so far as he is Celtic, he has snatches of quick instinct which often make him feel he is fumbling, show him visions of an easier, more dexterous behaviour, disconcert him and fill him with misgiving. No people, therefore, are so shy, so self-conscious, so embarrassed as the English, because two natures are mixed in them, and natures which pull them such different ways. The Germanic part, indeed, triumphs in us, we are a Germanic people; but not so wholly as to exclude hauntings of Celtism, which clash with our Germanism, producing, as I believe, our *humour*, neither German nor Celtic, and so affect us that we strike people as odd and singular, not to be referred to any known type, and like nothing but ourselves. 'Nearly every Englishman,' says an excellent and by no means unfriendly observer, George Sand, 'nearly every Englishman, however good-looking he may be, has always something singular about him which easily comes to seem comic;—a sort of typical awkwardness (*gaucherie typique*) in his looks or appearance, which hardly ever wears out.' I say this strangeness is accounted for by the English nature being mixed as we have seen, while the Latin nature is all of a piece, and so is the German nature, and the Celtic nature.

It is impossible to go very fast when the matter with which one has to deal, besides being new and little explored, is also by its nature so subtle, eluding one's grasp unless one handles it with all possible delicacy and care. It is in our poetry that the Celtic part in us has left its trace clearest, and in our poetry I must follow it before I have done.

VI.

If I were asked where English poetry got these three things, its turn for style, its turn for melancholy, and its turn for natural magic, for catching and rendering the charm of nature in a wonderfully near and vivid way,—I should answer, with some doubt, that it got much of its turn for style from a Celtic source; with less doubt, that it got much of its melancholy from a Celtic source; with no doubt at all, that from a Celtic source it got nearly all its natural magic.

Any German with penetration and tact in matters of literary criticism will own that the principal deficiency of German poetry is in style; that for style, in the highest sense, it shows but little feeling. Take the eminent masters of style, the poets who best give the idea of what the peculiar power which lies in style is, Pindar, Virgil, Dante, Milton. An example of the peculiar effect which these poets produce, you can hardly give from German poetry. Examples enough you can give from German poetry of the effect produced by genius, thought, and feeling expressing themselves in clear language, simple language, passionate language, eloquent language, with harmony and melody; but not of the peculiar effect exercised by eminent power of style. Every reader of Dante can at once call to mind what the peculiar effect I mean is; I spoke of it in my lectures on translating Homer, and there I took an example of it from Dante, who perhaps manifests it more eminently than any other poet. But from Milton, too, one may take examples of it abundantly; compare this from Milton:—

> . . . nor sometimes forget
> Those other two equal with me in fate,
> So were I equall'd with them in renown,
> Blind Thamyris and blind Mæonides—

with this from Goethe:—

> Es bildet ein Talent sich in der Stille,
> Sich ein Character in dem Strom der Welt.

Nothing can be better in its way than the style in which Goethe there presents his thought, but it is the style of prose as much as of poetry; it is lucid, harmonious, earnest, eloquent, but it has not received that peculiar kneading, heightening, and re-casting which is observable in the style of the passage from Milton,—a style which seems to have for its cause a certain pressure of emotion, and an ever-surging, yet bridled, excitement in the poet, giving a special intensity to his way of delivering himself. In poetical races and epochs this turn for style is peculiarly observable; and perhaps it is only on condition of having this somewhat heightened and difficult manner, so different from the plain manner of prose, that poetry gets the privilege of being loosed, at its best moments, into that perfectly simple, limpid style, which is the supreme style of all, but the simplicity of which is still not the simplicity of prose. The simplicity of Menander's style is the simplicity of prose, and is the same kind of simplicity as that which Goethe's style, in the passage I have quoted, exhibits; but Menander does not belong to a great poetical moment, he comes too late for it; it is the simple passages in poets like Pindar or Dante which are perfect, being masterpieces of *poetical* simplicity. One may say the same of the simple passages in Shakspeare; they are perfect, their simplicity being a *poetical* simplicity. They are the golden, easeful, crowning moments of a manner which is always pitched in another key from that of prose; a manner changed and heightened; the Elizabethan style, regnant in most of our dramatic poetry to this day, is mainly the continuation of this manner of Shakspeare's. It was a manner much more turbid and strewn with blemishes than the manner of Pindar, Dante, or Milton; often it was detestable; but it owed its existence to Shakspeare's instinctive impulse towards *style* in poetry, to his native sense of the necessity for it; and without the basis of style everywhere, faulty though it may in some places be, we should not have had the beauty of expression, unsurpassable for effectiveness and charm, which is reached in Shakspeare's best passages. The turn for style is perceptible all through English poetry, proving, to my mind, the genuine poetical gift of the race; this turn imparts to our poetry a stamp of high distinction, and sometimes it doubles the force of a poet not by nature of the very highest order, such as Gray, and raises him to a rank beyond what his natural richness and power seem to promise. Goethe, with his fine critical perception, saw clearly enough both the power of style in itself, and the lack of style in the literature of his own country; and perhaps if we regard him solely as a German, not as a European, his great work was that he laboured all his life to impart style into German literature, and firmly to establish it there. Hence the immense importance to him of the world of classical art, and of the productions of Greek or Latin genius, where style so eminently manifests its power. Had he found in the German genius and literature an element of style existing by nature and ready to his hand, half his work, one may say, would have been saved him, and he might have done much more in poetry. But as it was, he had to try and create out of his own powers, a style for German poetry, as well as to provide contents for this style to carry; and thus his labour as a poet was doubled.

It is to be observed that power of style, in the sense in which I am here speaking of style, is something quite different from the power of idiomatic, simple, nervous, racy expression, such as the expression of healthy, robust natures so often is, such as Luther's was in a striking degree. Style, in my sense of the word, is a peculiar re-casting and heightening, under a certain condition of spiritual excitement, of what a man has to say, in such a manner as to add dignity and distinction to it; and dignity and distinction are not terms which suit many acts or words of Luther. Deeply touched with the *Gemeinheit* which is the bane of his nation, as he is at the same time a grand example of the honesty which is his nation's excellence, he can seldom even show himself brave, resolute and truthful, without showing a strong dash of coarseness and commonness all the while; the right definition of Luther, as of our own Bunyan, is that he is a Philistine of genius. So Luther's sincere idiomatic German,—such language is this: 'Hilf lieber Gott, wie manchen Jammer habe ich gesehen, dass der gemeine Mann doch so gar nichts weiss von der christlichen Lehre!'—no more proves a power of style in German literature, than Cobbett's sinewy idiomatic English proves it in English literature. Power of style, properly so-called, as manifested in masters of style like Dante or Milton in poetry, Cicero, Bossuet or Bolingbroke in prose, is something quite different, and has, as I have said, for its characteristic effect, this: to add dignity and distinction.

Style, then, the Germans are singularly without, and it is strange that the power of style should show itself so strongly as it does in the Icelandic poetry, if the Scandinavians are such genuine Teutons as is commonly supposed. Fauriel used to talk of the Scandinavian Teutons and the German Teutons, as if they were two divisions of the same people, and the common notion about them, no doubt, is very much this. Since the war in Schleswig-Holstein, however, all one's German friends are exceedingly anxious to insist on the difference of nature between themselves and the Scandinavians; when one expresses surprise that the German sense of nationality should be so deeply affronted by the rule over Germans, not of Latins or Celts, but of brother Teutons or next door to it, a German will give you I know not how long a catalogue of the radical points of unlikeness, in genius and disposition, between himself and a Dane. This emboldens me to remark that there is a fire, a sense of style, a distinction, in Icelandic poetry, which German poetry has not. Icelandic poetry, too, shows a powerful and developed technic; and I wish to throw out, for examination by those who are competent to sift the matter, the suggestion that this power of style and development of technic in the Norse poetry seems to point towards an early Celtic influence or intermixture. It is curious that Zeuss, in his grammar, quotes a text which gives countenance to this notion; as late as the ninth century, he says, there were Irish Celts in Iceland; and the text he quotes to show this, is as follows:—'In 870 A.D., when the Norwegians came to Iceland, there were Christians there, who departed, and left behind them Irish books, bells, and other things; from whence it may be inferred that these Christians were Irish.' I speak, and ought to speak, with the utmost diffidence on all these questions of ethnology; but I must say that when I read this text in Zeuss, I caught eagerly at the clue it seemed to offer; for I had been hearing the *Nibelungen* read and commented on in German schools (German schools have the good habit of reading and commenting on German poetry, as we read and comment on Homer and Virgil, but do *not* read and comment on Chaucer and Shakspeare), and it struck me how the fatal humdrum and want of style of the Germans had marred their way of telling this magnificent tradition of the *Nibelungen*, and taken half its grandeur and power out of it; while in the Icelandic poems which deal with this tradition, its grandeur and power are much more fully visible, and everywhere in the poetry of the Edda there is a force of style and a distinction as unlike as possible to the want of both in the German *Nibelungen*.[15] At the same time the Scandinavians have a realism, as it is called, in their genius, which abundantly proves their relationship with the Germans; any one whom Mr. Dasent's delightful books have made acquainted with the prose tales of the Norsemen, will be struck with the stamp of a Teutonic nature in them; but the Norse poetry seems to have something which from Teutonic sources alone it could not have derived; which the Germans have not, and which the Celts have.

This something is *style*, and the Celts certainly have it in a wonderful measure. Style is the most striking quality of their poetry. Celtic poetry seems to make up to

[15] Lord Strangford's note on this is:—'The Irish monks whose bells and books were found in Iceland could not have contributed anything to the old Norse spirit, for they had perished before the first Norseman had set foot on the island. The form of the old Norse poetry known to us as Icelandic, from the accident of its preservation in that island alone, is surely Pan-Teutonic from old times; the ar and method of its strictly literary cultivation must have been much influenced by the contemporary Old-English national poetry, with which the Norsemen were in constant contact; and its larger, freer, and wilder spirit must have been owing to their freer and wilder life, to say nothing of their roused and warring paganism. They could never have known any Celts save when living in embryo with other Teutons.'

Very likely Lord Strangford is right, but the proposition with which he begins is at variance with what the text quoted by Zeuss alleges.

itself for being unable to master the world and give an adequate interpretation of it, by throwing all its force into style, by bending language at any rate to its will, and expressing the ideas it has with unsurpassable intensity, elevation, and effect. It has all through it a sort of intoxication of style,—a *Pindarism*, to use a word formed from the name of the poet, on whom, above all other poets, the power of style seems to have exercised an inspiring and intoxicating effect; and not in its great poets only, in Taliesin, or Llywarch Hen, or Ossian, does the Celtic genius show this Pindarism, but in all its productions:—

> The grave of March is this, and this the grave of Gwythyr;
> Here is the grave of Gwgawn Gleddyfreidd;
> But unknown is the grave of Arthur.

That comes from the Welsh *Memorials of the Graves of the Warriors*, and if we compare it with the familiar memorial inscriptions of an English churchyard (for we English have so much Germanism in us that our productions offer abundant examples of German want of style as well as of its opposite):—

> Afflictions sore long time I bore,
> Physicians were in vain,
> Till God did please Death should me seize
> And ease me of my pain—

if, I say, we compare the Welsh memorial lines with the English, which in their *Gemeinheit* of style are truly Germanic, we shall get a clear sense of what that Celtic talent for style I have been speaking of is.

Or take this epitaph of an Irish Celt, Angus the Culdee, whose *Féliré*, or festology, I have already mentioned; a festology in which, at the end of the eighth or beginning of the ninth century, he collected from 'the countless hosts of the illuminated books of Erin' (to use his own words) the festivals of the Irish saints, his poem having a stanza for every day in the year. The epitaph on Angus, who died at Cluain Eidhnech, in Queen's County, runs thus:—

> Angus in the assembly of Heaven,
> Here are his tomb and his bed;
> It is from hence he went to death,
> In the Friday, to holy Heaven.
>
> It was in Cluain Eidhnech he was rear'd;
> It was in Cluain Eidhnech he was buried;
> In Cluain Eidhnech, of many crosses,
> He first read his psalms.

That is by no eminent hand; and yet a Greek epitaph could not show a finer perception of what constitutes propriety and felicity of style in compositions of this nature. Take the well-known Welsh prophecy about the fate of the Britons:—

> Their Lord they will praise,
> Their speech they will keep,
> Their land they will lose,
> Except wild Wales.

To however late an epoch that prophecy belongs, what a feeling for style, at any rate, it manifests! And the same thing may be said of the famous Welsh triads. We may put aside all the vexed questions as to their greater or less antiquity, and still what important witness they bear to the genius for literary style of the people who produced them!

Now we English undoubtedly exhibit very often the want of sense for style of our German kinsmen. The churchyard lines I just now quoted afford an instance of it: but the whole branch of our literature,—and a very popular branch it is, our hymnology,—to which those lines are to be referred, is one continued instance of it. Our German kinsmen and we are the great people for hymns. The Germans are very proud of their hymns, and we are very proud of ours; but it is hard to say which of the two, the German hymn-book or ours, has least poetical worth in itself, or does least to prove genuine poetical power in the people producing it. I have not a word to say against Sir Roundell Palmer's choice and arrangement of materials for his *Book of Praise*; I am content to put them on a level (and that is giving them the highest possible rank) with Mr. Palgrave's choice and arrangement of materials for his *Golden Treasury*; but yet no sound critic can doubt that, so far as poetry is concerned, while the *Golden Treasury* is a monument of a nation's strength, the *Book of Praise* is a monument of a nation's weakness. Only the German race, with its want of quick instinctive tact, of delicate, sure perception, could have invented the hymn as the Germans and we have it; and our non-German turn for style,—style, of which the very essence is a certain happy fineness and truth of poetical perception,—could not but desert us when our German nature carried us into a kind of composition which can please only when the perception is somewhat blunt. Scarcely any one of us ever judges our hymns fairly, because works of this kind have two sides,—their side for religion and their side for poetry. Everything which has helped a man in his religious life, everything which associates itself in his mind with the growth of that life, is beautiful and venerable to him; in this way, productions of little or no poetical value, like the German hymns and ours, may come to be regarded as very precious. Their worth in this sense, as means by which we have been edified, I do not for a moment hold cheap; but there is an edification proper to all our stages of development, the highest as well as the lowest, and it is for man to press on towards the highest stages of his development, with the certainty that for those stages, too, means of edification will not be found wanting. Now certainly it is a higher state of development when our fineness of perception is keen than when it is blunt. And if,—whereas the Semitic genius placed its highest spiritual life in the religious sentiment, and made that the basis of its poetry,—the Indo-European genius places its highest spiritual life in the imaginative reason, and makes that the basis of its poetry, we are none the better for wanting the perception to discern a natural law, which is, after all, like every natural law, irresistible; we are none the better for trying to make ourselves Semitic, when Nature has made us Indo-European, and to shift the basis of our poetry. We may mean well; all manner of good may happen to us on the road we go; but we are not on our real right road, the road we must in the end follow.

That is why, when our hymns betray a false tendency by losing a power which accompanies the poetical work of our race on our other more suitable lines, the indication thus given is of great value and instructiveness for us. One of our main gifts for poetry deserts us in our hymns, and so gives us a hint as to the one true basis for the spiritual work of an Indo-European people, which the Germans, who have not this particular gift of ours, do not and cannot get in this way, though they may get it in others. It is worth noticing that the masterpieces of the spiritual work of Indo-Europeans, taking the pure religious sentiment, and not the imaginative reason, for their basis, are works like the *Imitation*, the *Dies Iræ*, the *Stabat Mater*—works clothing themselves in the middle-age Latin, the genuine native voice of no Indo-European nation. The perfection of their kind, but that kind not perfectly legitimate, they take a language not perfectly legitimate; as if to show, that when mankind's Semitic age is once passed, the age which produced the great incomparable monuments of the pure religious sentiment, the books of Job and Isaiah, the Psalms,—works truly to be called inspired, because the same divine power which worked in those who produced them works no longer,—as if to show us, that, after this primitive age, we Indo-Europeans must feel these works without attempting to re-make them; and that our poetry, if it tries to make itself simply the organ of the religious sentiment, leaves the true course, and must conceal this by not speaking a living language. The moment it speaks a living language, and still makes itself the organ of the religious sentiment only, as in the German and English hymns, it betrays weakness;—the weakness of all false tendency.

But if by attending to the Germanism in us English and to its works, one has come to doubt whether we, too, are not thorough Germans by genius and with the German deadness to style, one has only to repeat to oneself a line of Milton,—a poet intoxicated with the passion for style as much as Taliesin or Pindar,—to see that we have another side to our genius beside the German one. Whence do we get it? The Normans may have brought in among us the Latin sense for rhetoric and style,—for, indeed, this sense goes naturally with a high spirit and a strenuousness like theirs,—but the sense for style which English poetry shows is something finer than we could well have got from a people so positive and so little poetical as the Normans; and it seems to me we may much more plausibly derive it from a root of the poetical Celtic nature in us.

Its chord of penetrating passion and melancholy, again, its *Titanism* as we see it in Byron,—what other European poetry possesses that like the English, and where do we get it from? The Celts, with their vehement reaction against the despotism of fact, with their sensuous nature, their manifold striving, their adverse destiny, their immense calamities, the Celts are the prime authors of this vein of piercing regret and passion,—of this Titanism in poetry. A famous book, Macpherson's *Ossian*, carried in the last century this vein like a flood of lava through Europe. I am not going to criticise Macpherson's *Ossian* here. Make the part of what is forged, modern, tawdry, spurious, in the book, as large as you please; strip Scotland, if you like, of every feather of borrowed plumes which on the strength of Macpherson's *Ossian* she may have stolen from that *vetus et major Scotia*, the true home of the Ossianic poetry, Ireland; I make no objection. But there will still be left in the book a residue with the very soul of the Celtic genius in it, and which has the proud distinction of having brought this soul of the Celtic genius into contact with the genius of the nations of modern Europe, and enriched all our poetry by it. Woody Morven, and echoing Sora, and Selma with its silent halls!—we all owe them a debt of gratitude, and when we are unjust enough to forget it, may the Muse forget us! Choose any one of the better passages in Macpherson's *Ossian* and you can see even at this time of day what an apparition of newness and power such a strain must have been to the eighteenth century:—

'I have seen the walls of Balclutha, but they were desolate. The fox looked out from the windows, the rank grass of the wall waved round her head. Raise the song of mourning, O bards, over the land of strangers. They have but fallen before us, for one day we must fall. Why dost thou build the hall, son of the winged days? Thou lookest from thy towers to-day; yet a few years, and the blast of the desert comes; it howls in thy empty court, and whistles round thy half-worn shield. Let the blast of the desert come! we shall be renowned in our day.'

All Europe felt the power of that melancholy; but what I wish to point out is, that no nation of Europe so caught in its poetry the passionate penetrating accent of the Celtic genius, its strain of Titanism, as the English. Goethe, like Napoleon, felt the spell of Ossian very powerfully, and he quotes a long passage from him in his *Werther*. But what is there Celtic, turbulent, and Titanic about the German Werther, that amiable, cultivated, and melancholy young man, having for his sorrow and suicide the perfectly definite motive that Lotte cannot be his? Faust, again, has nothing unaccountable, defiant and Titanic in him; his knowledge does not bring him the satisfaction he expected from it, and meanwhile he finds himself poor and growing old, and baulked of the palpable enjoyment of life; and here is the motive for Faust's discontent. In the most energetic and impetuous of Goethe's creations,—his *Prometheus*,—it is not Celtic self-will and passion, it is rather the Germanic sense of justice and reason, which revolts against the despotism of Zeus. The German *Sehnsucht* itself is a wistful, soft, tearful longing, rather than a struggling, fierce, passionate one. But the Celtic melancholy is struggling, fierce, passionate; to catch its note, listen to Llywarch Hen in old age, addressing his crutch:—

> O my crutch! is it not autumn, when the fern is red, the water-flag yellow? Have I not hated that which I love?
>
> O my crutch! is it not winter-time now, when men talk together after that they have drunken? Is not the side of my bed left desolate?
>
> O my crutch! is it not spring, when the cuckoo passes through the air, when the foam sparkles on the sea? The young maidens no longer love me.
>
> O my crutch! is it not the first day of May? The furrows, are they not shining; the young corn, is it not springing? Ah! the sight of thy handle makes me wroth.
>
> O my crutch! stand straight, thou wilt support me the better; it is very long since I was Llywarch.

> Behold old age, which makes sport of me, from the hair of my head to my teeth, to my eyes, which women loved.
>
> The four things I have all my life most hated fall upon me together,—coughing and old age, sickness and sorrow.
>
> I am old, I am alone, shapeliness and warmth are gone from me; the couch of honour shall be no more mine: I am miserable, I am bent on my crutch.
>
> How evil was the lot allotted to Llywarch, the night when he was brought forth! sorrows without end, and no deliverance from his burden.

There is the Titanism of the Celt, his passionate, turbulent, indomitable reaction against the despotism of fact; and of whom does it remind us so much as of Byron?

> The fire which on my bosom preys
> Is lone as some volcanic isle;
> No torch is kindled at its blaze;
> A funeral pile!

Or, again:—

> Count o'er the joys thine hours have seen,
> Count o'er thy days from anguish free,
> And know, whatever thou hast been,
> 'Tis something better not to be.

One has only to let one's memory begin to fetch passages from Byron striking the same note as that passage from Llywarch Hen, and she will not soon stop. And all Byron's heroes, not so much in collision with outward things, as breaking on some rock of revolt and misery in the depths of their own nature; Manfred, self-consumed, fighting blindly and passionately with I know not what, having nothing of the consistent development and intelligible motive of Faust,—Manfred, Lara, Cain, what are they but Titanic? Where in European poetry are we to find this Celtic passion of revolt so warm-breathing, puissant, and sincere; except perhaps in the creation of a yet greater poet than Byron, but an English poet, too, like Byron,—in the Satan of Milton?

> . . . What though the field be lost?
> All is not lost; the unconquerable will,
> And study of revenge, immortal hate,
> And courage never to submit or yield,
> And what is else not to be overcome.

There, surely, speaks a genius to whose composition the Celtic fibre was not wholly a stranger!

And as, after noting the Celtic Pindarism or power of style present in our poetry, we noted the German flatness coming in in our hymns, and found here a proof of our compositeness of nature; so, after noting the Celtic Titanism or power of rebellious passion in our poetry, we may also note the Germanic patience and reasonableness in it, and get in this way a second proof how mixed a spirit we have. After Llywarch Hen's:—

> How evil was the lot allotted to Llywarch, the night when he was brought forth

after Byron's:—

> Count o'er the joys thine hours have seen—

take this of Southey's, in answer to the question whether he would like to have his youth over again:—

> Do I regret the past?
> Would I live o'er again
> The morning hours of life?
> Nay, William, nay, not so!
> Praise be to God who made me what I am,
> Other I would not be.

There we have the other side of our being; the Germanic goodness, docility, and fidelity to nature, in place of the Celtic Titanism.

The Celt's quick feeling for what is noble and distinguished gave his poetry style; his indomitable personality gave it pride and passion; his sensibility and nervous exaltation gave it a better gift still, the gift of rendering with wonderful felicity the magical charm of nature. The forest solitude, the bubbling spring, the wild flowers, are everywhere in romance. They have a mysterious life and grace there; they are nature's own children, and utter her secret in a way which makes them something quite different from the woods, waters, and plants of Greek and Latin poetry. Now of this delicate magic, Celtic romance is so pre-eminent a mistress, that it seems impossible to believe the power did not come into romance from the Celts.[16] Magic is just the word for it,—the magic of nature; not merely the beauty of nature,—that the Greeks and Latins had; not merely an honest smack of the soil, a faithful realism,—that the Germans had; but the intimate life of nature, her weird power and her fairy charm. As the Saxon names of places, with the pleasant wholesome smack of the soil in them,—Weathersfield, Thaxted, Shalford,—are to the Celtic names of places, with their penetrating, lofty beauty,—Velindra, Tyntagel, Caernarvon,—so is the homely realism of German and Norse nature to the fairy-like loveliness of Celtic nature. Gwydion wants a wife for his pupil: 'Well,' says Math, 'we will seek, I and thou, by charms and illusions, to form a wife for him out of flowers. So they took the blossoms of the oak, and the blossoms of the broom, and the blossoms of the meadow-sweet, and produced from them a maiden, the fairest and most graceful that man ever saw. And they baptized her, and gave her the name of Flower-Aspect.' Celtic romance is full of exquisite touches like that, showing the delicacy of the Celt's feeling in these matters, and how deeply nature lets him come into her secrets. The quick dropping

[16] Rhyme,—the most striking characteristic of our modern poetry as distinguished from that of the ancients, and a main source, to our poetry, of its magic and charm, of what we call its *romantic element,*—rhyme itself, all the weight of evidence tends to show, comes into our poetry from the Celts.

of blood is called 'faster than the fall of the dewdrop from the blade of reed-grass upon the earth, when the dew of June is at the heaviest.' And thus is Olwen described: 'More yellow was her hair than the flower of the broom, and her skin was whiter than the foam of the wave, and fairer were her hands and her fingers than the blossoms of the wood-anemony amidst the spray of the meadow fountains.' For loveliness it would be hard to beat that; and for magical clearness and nearness take the following:—

'And in the evening Peredur entered a valley, and at the head of the valley he came to a hermit's cell, and the hermit welcomed him gladly, and there he spent the night. And in the morning he arose, and when he went forth, behold, a shower of snow had fallen the night before, and a hawk had killed a wild-fowl in front of the cell. And the noise of the horse scared the hawk away, and a raven alighted upon the bird. And Peredur stood and compared the blackness of the raven, and the whiteness of the snow, and the redness of the blood, to the hair of the lady whom best he loved, which was blacker than the raven, and to her skin, which was whiter than the snow, and to her two cheeks, which were redder than the blood upon the snow appeared to be.'

And this, which is perhaps less striking, is not less beautiful:—

'And early in the day Geraint and Enid left the wood, and they came to an open country, with meadows on one hand and mowers mowing the meadows. And there was a river before them, and the horses bent down and drank the water. And they went up out of the river by a steep bank, and there they met a slender stripling with a satchel about his neck; and he had a small blue pitcher in his hand, and a bowl on the mouth of the pitcher.'

And here the landscape, up to this point so Greek in its clear beauty, is suddenly magicalised by the romance touch:—

'And they saw a tall tree by the side of the river, one-half of which was in flames from the root to the top, and the other half was green and in full leaf.'

Magic is the word to insist upon,—a magically vivid and near interpretation of nature; since it is this which constitutes the special charm and power of the effect I am calling attention to, and it is for this that the Celt's sensibility gives him a peculiar aptitude. But the matter needs rather fine handling, and it is easy to make mistakes here in our criticism. In the first place, Europe tends constantly to become more and more one community, and we tend to become Europeans instead of merely Englishmen, Frenchmen, Germans, Italians; so whatever aptitude or felicity one people imparts into spiritual work, gets imitated by the others, and thus tends to become the common property of all. Therefore anything so beautiful and attractive as the natural magic I am speaking of, is sure, now-a-days, if it appears in the productions of the Celts, or of the English, or of the French, to appear in the productions of the Germans also, or in the productions of the Italians; but there will be a stamp of perfectness and inimitableness about it in the literatures where it is native, which it will not have in the literatures where it is not native. Novalis or Rückert, for instance, have their eye fixed on nature, and have undoubtedly a feeling for natural magic; a rough-and-ready critic easily credits them and the Germans with the Celtic fineness of tact, the Celtic nearness to nature and her secret; but the question is whether the strokes in the German's picture of nature[17] have ever the indefinable delicacy, charm, and perfection of the Celt's touch in the pieces I just now quoted, or of Shakspeare's touch in his daffodil, Wordsworth's in his cuckoo, Keats's in his Autumn, Obermann's in his mountain birch-tree, or his Easter-daisy among the Swiss farms. To decide where the gift for natural magic originally lies, whether it is properly Celtic or Germanic, we must decide this question.

In the second place, there are many ways of handling nature, and we are here only concerned with one of them; but a rough-and-ready critic imagines that it is all the same so long as nature is handled at all, and fails to draw the needful distinction between modes of handling her. But these modes are many; I will mention four of them now: there is the conventional way of handling nature, there is the faithful way of handling nature, there is the Greek way of handling nature, there is the magical way of handling nature. In all these three last the eye is on the object, but with a difference; in the faithful way of handling nature, the eye is on the object, and that is all you can say; in the Greek, the eye is on the object, but lightness and brightness are added; in the magical, the eye is on the object, but charm and magic are added. In the conventional way of handling nature, the eye is not on the object; what that means we all know, we have only to think of our eighteenth-century poetry:—

> As when the moon, refulgent lamp of night—

to call up any number of instances. Latin poetry supplies plenty of instances too; if we put this from Propertius's *Hylas*:—

> . . . manus heroum . . .
> Mollia composita litora fronde togit—

side by side with the line of Theocritus by which it was suggested:—

> *λειμὼν γάρ σφιν ἔκειτο μέγας, στιβάδεσσιν ὄνειαρ*—

we get at the same moment a good specimen both of the conventional and of the Greek way of handling nature. But from our own poetry we may get specimens of the Greek way of handling nature, as well as of the conventional: for instance, Keats's:—

> What little town by river or seashore,

[17] Take the following attempt to render the natural magic supposed to pervade Tieck's poetry:—'In diesen Dichtungen herrscht eine geheimnissvolle Innigkeit, ein sonderbares Einverständniss mit der Natur, besonders mit der Pflanzen—und Steinreich. Der Leser fühlt sich da wie in einem verzauberten Walde; er hört die unterirdischen Quellen melodisch rauschen; wildfremde Wunderblumen schauen ihn an mit ihren bunten schnsüchtigen Augen; unsichtbare Lippen küssen seine Wangen mit neckender Zärtlichkeit; *hohe Pilze, wie goldne Glocken, wachsen klingend empor am Fusse der Bäume;*' and so on. Now that stroke of the *hohe Pilze*, the great funguses, would have been impossible to the tact and delicacy of a born lover of nature like the Celt, and could only have come from a German who has *hineinstudirt* himself into natural magic. It is a crying false note, which carries us at once out of the world of nature-magic and the breath of the woods, into the world of theatre-magic and the smell of gas and orange-peel.

Or mountain-built with quiet citadel,
Is emptied of its folk, this pious morn?

is Greek, as Greek as a thing from Homer or Theocritus; it is composed with the eye on the object, a radiancy and light clearness being added. German poetry abounds in specimens of the faithful way of handling nature; an excellent example is to be found in the stanzas called *Zueignung*, prefixed to Goethe's poems; the morning walk, the mist, the dew, the sun, are as faithful as they can be, they are given with the eye on the object, but there the merit of the work, as a handling of nature, stops; neither Greek radiance nor Celtic magic is added; the power of these is not what gives the poem in question its merit, but a power of quite another kind, a power of moral and spiritual emotion. But the power of Greek radiance Goethe could give to his handling of nature, and nobly too, as any one who will read his *Wanderer*,—the poem in which a wanderer falls in with a peasant woman and her child by their hut, built out of the ruins of a temple near Cuma,—may see. Only the power of natural magic Goethe does not, I think, give; whereas Keats passes at will from the Greek power to that power which is, as I say, Celtic; from his:—

What little town, by river or seashore—

to his:—

White hawthorn and the pastoral eglantine,
Fast-fading violets cover'd up in leaves—

or his:—

. . . magic casements, opening on the foam
Of perilous seas, in fairy lands forlorn—

in which the very same note is struck as in those extracts which I quoted from Celtic romance, and struck with authentic and unmistakeable power.

Shakspeare, in handling nature, touches this Celtic note so exquisitely, that perhaps one is inclined to be always looking for the Celtic note in him, and not to recognise his Greek note when it comes. But if one attends well to the difference between the two notes, and bears in mind, to guide one, such things as Virgil's 'moss-grown springs and grass softer than sleep:'—

Muscosi fontes et somno mollior herba—

as his charming flower-gatherer, who—

Pallentes violas et summa papavera carpens
Narcissum et florem jungit bene olentis anethi—

as his quinces and chestnuts:—

. . . cana legam tenera lanugine mala
Castaneasque nuces . . .

then, I think, we shall be disposed to say that in Shakspeare's—

I know a bank where the wild thyme blows,
Where oxlips and the nodding violet grows,
Quite over-canopied with luscious woodbine,

With sweet musk-roses and with eglantine—

it is mainly a Greek note which is struck. Then, again in his:—

. . . look how the floor of heaven
Is thick inlaid with patines of bright gold!

we are at the very point of transition from the Greek note to the Celtic; there is the Greek clearness and brightness, with the Celtic aërialness and magic coming in. Then we have the sheer, inimitable Celtic note in passages like this:—

Met we on hill, in dale, forest or mead,
By paved fountain or by rushy brook,
Or in the beached margent of the sea—

or this, the last I will quote:—

The moon shines bright. In such a night as this,
When the sweet wind did gently kiss the trees,
And they did make no noise, in such a night
Troilus, methinks, mounted the Trojan walls—

. . . in such a night
Did Thisbe fearfully o'ertrip the dew—

. . . in such a night
Stood Dido, with a willow in her hand,
Upon the wild sea-banks, and waved her love
To come again to Carthage.

And those last lines of all are so drenched and intoxicated with the fairy-dew of that natural magic which is our theme, that I cannot do better then end with them.

And now, with the pieces of evidence in our hand, let us go to those who say it is vain to look for Celtic elements in any Englishman, and let us ask them, first, if they seize what we mean by the power of natural magic in Celtic poetry; secondly, if English poetry does not eminently exhibit this power; and, thirdly, where they suppose English poetry got it from?

I perceive that I shall be accused of having rather the air, in what I have said, of denying this and that gift to the Germans, and of establishing our difference from them a little ungraciously and at their expense. The truth is, few people have any real care to analyse closely in their criticism; they merely employ criticism as a means for heaping all praise on what they like, and all blame on what they dislike. Those of us (and they are many) who owe a great debt of gratitude to the German spirit and to German literature, do not like to be told of any powers being lacking there; we are like the young ladies who think the hero of their novel is only half a hero unless he has all perfections united in him. But nature does not work, either in heroes or races, according to the young ladies' notion. We all are what we are, the hero and the great nation are what they are, by our limitations as well as by our powers, by lacking something as well as by possessing something. It is not always gain to possess this or that gift, or loss to lack this or that gift. Our great, our only first-rate body of contemporary poetry is the German; the grand business of modern poetry,—a moral interpretation, from an independent point of view, of man and the world,—it is only German poetry, Goethe's poetry, that has, since the Greeks, made much way with. Campbell's power of style, and the natural magic of Keats and Wordsworth, and Byron's Titanic personality, may be wanting to this poetry; but see what it has accomplished without them! How much more than Campbell with his power of style, and Keats and Wordsworth with their natural magic, and Byron with his Titanic personality! Why, for the immense serious task it had to perform, the steadiness of German poetry, its going near the ground, its patient fidelity to nature, its using great plainness of speech, poetical drawbacks in one point of view, were safeguards and helps in another. The plainness and earnestness of the two lines I have already quoted from Goethe:—

> Es bildet ein Talent sich in der Stille,
> Sich ein Character in dem Strom der Welt—

compared with the play and power of Shakspeare's style or Dante's, suggest at once the difference between Goethe's task and theirs, and the fitness of the faithful laborious German spirit for its own task. Dante's task was to set forth the lesson of the world from the point of view of mediæval Catholicism; the basis of spiritual life was given, Dante had not to make this anew. Shakspeare's task was to set forth the spectacle of the world when man's spirit re-awoke to the possession of the world at the Renaissance. The spectacle of human life, left to bear its own significance and tell its own story, but shown in all its fulness, variety, and power, is at that moment the great matter; but, if we are to press deeper, the basis of spiritual life is still at that time the traditional religion, reformed or unreformed, of Christendom, and Shakspeare has not to supply a new basis. But when Goethe came, Europe had lost her basis of spiritual life; she had to find it again; Goethe's task was,—the inevitable task for the modern poet henceforth is,—as it was for the Greek poet in the days of Pericles, not to preach a sublime sermon on a given text like Dante, not to exhibit all the kingdoms of human life and the glory of them like Shakspeare, but to interpret human life afresh, and to supply a new spiritual basis to it. This is not only a work for style, eloquence, charm, poetry; it is a work for science; and the scientific, serious German spirit, not carried away by this and that intoxication of ear, and eye, and self-will, has peculiar aptitudes for it.

We, on the other hand, do not necessarily gain by the commixture of elements in us; we have seen how the clashing of natures in us hampers and embarrasses our behaviour; we might very likely be more attractive, we might very likely be more successful, if we were all of a piece. Our want of sureness of taste, our eccentricity, come in great measure, no doubt, from our not being all of a piece, from our having no fixed, fatal, spiritual centre of gravity. The Rue de Rivoli is one thing, and Nuremberg is another, and Stonehenge is another; but we have a turn for all three, and lump them all up together. Mr. Tom Taylor's translations from Breton poetry offer a good example of this mixing; he has a genuine feeling for these Celtic matters, and often, as in the *Evil Tribute of Nomenoë*, or in *Lord Nann and the Fairy*, he is, both in movement and expression, true and appropriate; but he has a sort of Teutonism and Latinism in him too, and so he cannot forbear mixing with his Celtic strain such disparates as:—

> 'Twas mirk, mirk night, and the water bright
> Troubled and drumlie flowed—

which is evidently Lowland-Scotchy; or as:—

> Foregad, but thou'rt an artful hand!

which is English-stagey; or as:—

> To Gradlon's daughter, bright of blee,
> Her lover he whispered tenderly—
> *Bethink thee, sweet Dahut! the key!*

which is Anacreontic in the manner of Tom Moore. Yes, it is not a sheer advantage to have several strings to one's bow! if we had been all German, we might have had the science of Germany; if we had been all Celtic, we might have been popular and agreeable; if we had been all Latinised, we might have governed Ireland as the French govern Alsace, without getting ourselves detested. But now we have Germanism enough to make us Philistines, and Normanism enough to make us imperious, and Celtism enough to make us self-conscious and awkward; but German fidelity to Nature, and Latin precision and clear reason, and Celtic quick-wittedness and spirituality, we fall short of. Nay, perhaps, if we are doomed to perish (Heaven avert the omen!), we shall perish by our Celtism, by our self-will and want of patience with ideas, our inability to see the way the world is going; and yet those very Celts, by our affinity with whom we are perishing, will be hating and upbraiding us all the time.

This is a somewhat unpleasant view to take of the matter; but if it is true, its being unpleasant does not make it any less true, and we are always the better for seeing the truth. What we here see is not the whole truth, however. So long as this mixed constitution of our nature possesses us, we pay it tribute and serve it; so soon as we possess it, it pays us tribute and serves us. So long as we are blindly and ignorantly rolled about by the forces of our nature, their contradiction baffles us and lames us; so soon as we have clearly discerned what they are, and begun to apply to them a law of measure, control, and guidance, they may be made to work for our good and to carry us forward. Then we may have the good of our German part, the good of our Latin part, the good of our Celtic part; and instead of one part clashing with the other, we may bring it in to continue and perfect the other, when the other has given us all the good it can yield, and by being pressed further, could only give us its faulty excess. Then we may use the German faithfulness to Nature to give us science, and to free us from insolence and self-will; we may use the Celtic quickness of perception to give us delicacy, and to free us from hardness and Philistinism; we may use the Latin decisiveness to give us strenuous clear method, and to free us from fumbling and idling. Already, in their untrained state, these elements give signs, in our life and literature, of their being present in us, and a kind of prophecy of what they could do for us if they were properly observed, trained, and applied. But this they have not yet been; we ride one force of our nature to death; we will be nothing but Anglo-Saxons in the Old World or in the New; and when our race has built Bold Street, Liverpool, and pronounced it very good, it hurries across the Atlantic, and builds Nashville, and Jacksonville, and Milledgeville, and thinks it is fulfilling the designs of Providence in an incomparable manner. But true Anglo-Saxons, simply and sincerely rooted in the German nature, we are not and cannot be; all we have accomplished by our onesidedness is to blur and confuse the natural basis in ourselves altogether, and to become something eccentric, unattractive, and inharmonious.

A man of exquisite intelligence and charming character, the late Mr. Cobden, used to fancy that a better acquaintance with the United States was the grand panacea for us; and once in a speech he bewailed the inattention of our seats of learning to them, and seemed to think that if our ingenuous youth at Oxford were taught a little less about Ilissus, and a little more about Chicago, we should all be the better for it. Chicago has its claims upon us, no doubt; but it is evident that from the point of view to which I have been leading, a stimulation of our Anglo-Saxonism, such as is intended by Mr. Cobden's proposal, does not appear the thing most needful for us; seeing our American brothers themselves have rather, like us, to try and moderate the flame of Anglo-Saxonism in their own breasts, than to ask us to clap the bellows to it in ours. So I am inclined to beseech Oxford, instead of expiating her over-addiction to the Ilissus by lectures on Chicago, to give us an expounder for a still more remote-looking object than the Ilissus,—the Celtic languages and literature. And yet why should I call it remote? if, as I have been labouring to show, in the spiritual frame of us English ourselves, a Celtic fibre, little as we may have ever thought of tracing it, lives and works. *Aliens in speech, in religion, in blood*! said Lord Lyndhurst; the philologists have set him right about the speech, the physiologists about the blood; and perhaps, taking religion in the wide but true sense of our whole spiritual activity, those who have followed what I have been saying here will think that the Celt is not so wholly alien to us in religion. But, at any rate, let us consider that of the shrunken and diminished remains of this great primitive race, all, with one insignificant exception, belongs to the English empire; only Brittany is not ours; we have Ireland, the Scotch Highlands, Wales, the Isle of Man, Cornwall. They are a part of ourselves, we are deeply interested in knowing them, they are deeply interested in being known by us; and yet in the great and rich universities of this great and rich country there is no chair of Celtic, there is no study or teaching of Celtic matters; those who want them must go abroad for them. It is neither right nor reasonable that this should be so. Ireland has had in the last half century a band of Celtic students,—a band with which death, alas! has of late been busy,—from whence Oxford or Cambridge might have taken an admirable professor of Celtic; and with the authority of a university chair, a great Celtic scholar, on a subject little known, and where all would have readily deferred to him, might have by this time doubled our facilities for knowing the Celt, by procuring for this country Celtic documents which were inaccessible here, and preventing the dispersion of others which were accessible. It is not much that the English Government does for science or literature; but if Eugene O'Curry, from a chair of Celtic at Oxford, had appealed to the Government to get him copies or the originals of the Celtic treasures in the Burgundian Library at Brussels, or in the library of St. Isidore's College at Rome, even the English Government could not well have refused him. The invaluable Irish manuscripts in the Stowe Library the late Sir Robert Peel proposed, in 1849, to buy for the British Museum; Lord Macaulay, one of the trustees of the Museum, declared, with the confident shallowness which makes him so admired by public speakers and leading-article writers, and so intolerable to all searchers for truth, that he saw nothing in the whole collection worth purchasing for the Museum, except the correspondence of Lord Melville on the American war. That is to say, this correspondence of Lord Melville's was the only thing in the collection about which Lord Macaulay himself knew or cared. Perhaps an Oxford or Cambridge professor of Celtic might have been allowed to make his voice heard, on a matter of Celtic manuscripts, even against Lord Macaulay. The manuscripts were bought by Lord Ashburnham, who keeps them shut up, and will let no one consult them (at least up to the date when O'Curry published his *Lectures* he did so), 'for fear an actual acquaintance with their contents should decrease their value as matter of curiosity at some future transfer or sale.' Who knows? Perhaps an Oxford professor of Celtic might have touched the flinty heart of Lord Ashburnham.

At this moment, when the narrow Philistinism which has long had things its own way in England, is showing its natural fruits, and we are beginning to feel ashamed, and uneasy, and alarmed at it; now, when we are becoming aware that we have sacrificed to Philistinism culture, and insight, and dignity, and acceptance, and weight among the nations, and hold on events that deeply concern us, and control of the future, and yet that it cannot even give us the fool's paradise it promised us, but is apt to break down, and to leave us with Mr. Roebuck's and Mr. Lowe's laudations of our matchless happiness, and the largest circulation in the world assured to the *Daily Telegraph*, for our only comfort; at such a moment it needs some moderation not to be attacking Philistinism by storm, but to mine it through such gradual means as the slow approaches of culture, and the introduction of chairs of Celtic. But the hard unintelligence, which is just now our bane, cannot be conquered by storm; it must be suppled and reduced by culture, by a growth in the variety, fulness, and sweetness of our spiritual life; and this end can only be reached by studying things that are outside of ourselves, and by studying them disinterestedly. Let us reunite ourselves with our better mind and with the world through science; and let it be one of our angelic revenges on the Philistines, who among their other sins are the guilty authors of Fenianism, to found at Oxford a chair of Celtic, and to send, through the gentle ministration of science, a message of peace to Ireland.

Lector House believes that a society develops through a two-fold approach of continuous learning and adaptation, which is derived from the study of classic literary works spread across the historic timeline of literature records. Therefore, we aim at reviving, repairing and redeveloping all those inaccessible or damaged but historically as well as culturally important literature across subjects so that the future generations may have an opportunity to study and learn from past works to embark upon a journey of creating a better future.

This book is a result of an effort made by Lector House towards making a contribution to the preservation and repair of original ancient works which might hold historical significance to the approach of continuous learning across subjects.

HAPPY READING & LEARNING!

LECTOR HOUSE

LECTOR HOUSE LLP

E-MAIL: info@lectorhouse.com

9 789356 146730

9 789356 146730

Printed by Libri Plureos GmbH in Hamburg,
Germany